For Rob
May ♡
the Fabulous
Housemates!
(on anyone you share digs
with!)

SHARING HOUSING

Annamarie Pluhar

May 2012

SHARING HOUSING

*A Guidebook for
Finding and Keeping
Good Housemates*

Annamarie Pluhar

BAUHAN PUBLISHING
PETERBOROUGH, NEW HAMPSHIRE
2011

Annamarie@sharinghousing.com
Http://www.sharinghousing.com

978-0-87233-143-3

Library of Congress Cataloging-in-Publication Data

Pluhar, Annamarie.
  Sharing housing : a guidebook for finding and keeping good housemates / by Annamarie Pluhar.
     p. cm.
  Includes bibliographical references.
  ISBN 978-0-87233-143-3 (pbk. : alk. paper)
  1. Roommates. 2. Shared housing. I. Title.

  HQ975.P58 2011
  646.70084--dc22
                        2011004223

Cover design by Henry James

Illustrations by Jefferson Thomas

Typeset in Monotype Dante and Gill Sans by
Kirsty Anderson

Printed in Canada

BAUHAN
PUBLISHINGLLC
7 MAIN STREET PETERBOROUGH NEW HAMPSHIRE 03458
603-567-4430
WWW.BAUHANPUBLISHING.COM

CONTENTS

Acknowledgements

The processes described in this book and the lessons about sharing housing are the culmination of years of experience. I have lived with many people, and without them there would not have been a book. There are some whose faces I remember but whose names are lost. There were some who were dreadful mistakes. Then there are the ones who became friends in the time we lived together. In Poughkeepsie, New York, my housemates were Alice, Ann, Joan, Judy, Melanie, and Sally. In Somerville, Massachusetts, I shared housing with John, Gerard, Jennifer, Jeannette, Eve, Chris, Abby, Noelle, Karen, Madeleine, Scott, and Robin. In the Washington, DC, area, there were John, Loretta, Debi, Robert, Tracy, Lisa, Dan, John, Celina, Geoffrey, Annette, Reed, Carl, Kevin, and Carlos. A special thanks to Chris for his guideline on the incest taboo. Thank you to all for our time together and what I have learned by living with you.

Many stories of real people living in shared housing come from interviews. I found the interviewees through word of mouth and HARO (Helpareporter. com™) queries. The interviewees were all so generous with their time and open about both their good arrangements and the mistakes that they had made. Many thanks to: Rachel Arment, iishana Artra, Brooke Billings, Mary Cain, Anne Campbell, Teresa Coates, Lisa Deiterich, Linda Friedman, Michelle Fryer, Ann Guo, Terry Jackson, Kirsten Klöber, Mike Machuk, Ryan Matzner, Meg of MegExpressions, Dina Koukos Persampire, Matt Quinney, Alexa Ritchie, Sharon Sakson, Deborah Shuman, Gillaine Smith, Chelsea Spangler, Claire Wilson, and Connie Woodberry. A few stories come from persons who requested anonymity.

I had amazing help in getting this book written. The ladies of Three Books, Lisa Sieverts and Samantha Bovat, read the first and second drafts, giving me both a weekly deadline and incredibly useful feedback. Aylette Jenness combed the manuscript thoroughly and made suggestions that improved the book immensely. Jefferson Thomas drew the illustrations adding some levity to the seriousness of the book. Deborah Shuman and Bob Sherwood provided their editing skills. I am deeply grateful for all these generous contributions of time and talent. I'm thrilled that this book is published locally by Bauhan Publishing and that Sarah and I found each other when we did. Thank you, everyone.

Preface

Most of my adult life I have lived in shared housing. I have been the home seeker, looking for a place to live, hoping someone would agree to have me move in. I have also been the householder, the one offering a place to the home seeker, sizing up an applicant and deciding whether this person is right for me. I have had great housemates and I've made mistakes. What I've learned about finding and keeping good housemates is that there is a definite process for finding the good ones, the ones you can live with comfortably and harmoniously.

Why Shared Housing?

In these difficult times of higher housing costs and lower earnings, sharing housing makes sense. According to the 2009 U.S. Census†, more than a quarter of the households in this country are single occupancy, for a total of 31.5 million Americans living alone. Some 6.6 million Americans live in households with people who aren't related to them.

This trend is growing, as single householders of all ages realize that with housemates they can make ends meet. For example, Mike in Tennessee is a divorced professional in his mid-30s with a large house he once shared with his wife. His housemates are two family men who moved to the area for jobs while their wives and children remain in their homes and communities. Mike says, "We are a lifeboat for each other." In New Jersey, Sharon is a former video producer with a big house who now has Nikki as a housemate. Nikki is an MBA entrepreneur with a food business. By sharing a house with Sharon she's saving money—money she can invest in her business. In Las Vegas‡, the local news carried a story about a senior citizen named Rita who is looking for a housemate to help her stay in her house. She didn't know how to advertise or screen a housemate. She needs this book. Imagine cutting the cost of your

† U.S. Census Bureau. America's Families and Living Arrangments, 2009. URL: http://www.census.gov/population/www/socdemo/hh-fam/cps2009.html.
‡ ABC, 13 Action News. "More seniors looking for housemates to help with the cost of living." Las Vegas, KNTV; February 18, 2010. URL: http://www.ktnv.com/Global/story.asp?S=12003006

housing and utilities by half or a third. How would that help your finances?

People who choose to share housing discover other benefits. Linda, a busy middle-aged professional with empty bedrooms vacated by grown children, had no thought of sharing her home until her goddaughter asked to move in and pay rent. Now, Linda bubbles with enthusiasm about how nice it is to share her space. "I love having young blood in the house." For Mike, who works from his home office, it "brings something; one can have those conversations that help you get out of yourself. Hibernating is a bit unnerving."

Sharon discovered companionship at meals. One evening, when Nikki was still a new housemate, Nikki announced that she had to start eating better and proceeded to cook two steaks, one for herself and one for Sharon. Now, Sharon doesn't cook and doesn't want to. She says, "If Nikki had asked me if she could make me a steak, I would have said no. But there it was. And it was delicious." So now, Nikki occasionally cooks dinner for the two of them. Sharon brings the wine.

My Experience

Like many people of my generation, I started living in shared housing after college and while working at entry-level jobs. In those two years, I had five housemates. I made mistakes, some of them very big. I remember one housemate who was so depressed she had no furniture in her room, and had one big pot on the stove into which she threw things to make a soup. It was disgusting. I had to ask her to move out. After graduate school I moved into a fabulous apartment with two friends, whom I convinced to leave their expensive apartments for shared housing. After each left for their own reasons, I continued to live there as housemates came and went. I was there for eight years. I finally left that apartment to move in with a boyfriend in a new city. When we broke up, I moved in with a friend and her three-year-old son, where I lived for a year. Then I bought a house, a house that was big on purpose, a house that required that I have two housemates, because I wanted to live with others. I like having someone to say hello to, and I like sharing the bills. I lived in that house for 10 years. Over the course of those years I had many housemates; some lived with me for years, some for months. So all together I've shared housing for 21 years with people who started out as strangers.

One day, a dear friend was lamenting the state of her finances. I suggested that she could rent a room in her house, and she wailed, "I don't know how to do that!" When pressed, she reminded me of her past bad experiences. I pointed out that she hadn't done a very good job in selecting those housemates and I offered to coach her. Together we found her a good housemate. That was when I realized that I had developed a process for finding good housemates.

About This Book

This book maps out the path from your original thought, "Maybe I should find a housemate," to actually living with one. Like a guidebook for tourism or hiking, this book describes the milestones and choices on the path. You will learn where the traps and snags are, as well as where the well-trodden and proven paths can be found. You will find stories about others who are sharing housing and the methods they have found that work for them.

Sharing housing, as discussed in this book, is not co-housing or an intentional community. Co-housing and other intentional communities form so that people may live according to a particular set of ideals. Some intentional communities have a religious or political purpose. That's not what this book is about. Nor is this book about "co-habitation," the phrase used for couples who live together and are not married.

Like finding a job, finding a good housemate is a process with definite steps and decisions. This book maps that process, with helpful advice about what to look for, what to avoid, and when specific actions need to be taken. There is also a blog, www.sharinghousing.com, where you can find the worksheets for downloading and more information about sharing housing. There is a section for asking specific questions. You can also tell others your success stories, thus encouraging others to take this step. Together, this book and the blog hold your hand as you find *your* good housemates—the ones with whom you will live in harmony and comfort.

Introduction

Do You Want to Share Housing?

Sharing housing is a *negotiated agreement* between adults about how they will live under the same roof. People share housing in cities, suburbs, and the country. They share ranch houses, townhouses, and apartments. They share expensive condominiums and cheap flats. There are as many variations as there are people, types of homes, and locations.

Sharing housing is for adults of any age and all circumstances—those in graduate school or retirees, working people, empty-nesters or single parents, professionals who have homes in one place and jobs elsewhere. Housemates can be of the same generation or of different generations. They might be the same or different in terms of gender, class, nationality, sexual orientation, race, and life circumstances. The variations are infinite. The purpose of this guidebook is to help you find the living situation that works for you.

This book is divided into three sections. Section I deals with the initial things you'll want to consider before beginning the search for a shared living situation. Section II outlines the steps to follow in order to find a housemate or a home to share. Section III describes the day-to-day issues that commonly arise in shared housing, pointing out the potential pitfalls and how to avoid them.

Reasons for Sharing Housing

Why would you want to share housing? The most common reason is that you need a place to live and you can't afford to live alone. Other reasons for sharing housing are additional income, social connection, extra hands, and living light on the earth.

Income

If you already have a home and can rent a room in your house or apartment, what difference would an extra $300–900 a month make in your life? It could be the difference between scraping by and being able to eat out occasionally. It might allow you to pay the mortgage and keep your house despite unemployment or the loss of an income earner. It might allow you to have a college fund for a child or to pay for an expensive hobby. Figuring out what you can charge or what you can pay is part of the discussions in Chapter 2, "Initial Decisions—The Householder" and Chapter 3, "Initial Decisions—The Home Seeker."

Social Connection

When you live with a housemate, you have someone to whom you can say hello and more. Conversations can be spontaneous and easy. You may talk about your day. You may choose to have a meal together. You may discover a common pleasure in playing cards or watching sports together. Or you may both prefer to have privacy and little interaction. What kind of housemate you have, to what extent you interact or have shared interests, is up to you. Chapter 4, "How Do You Want to Live?" guides you through thinking about your selection process.

People who live alone tend to spend a lot of time alone and are often lonely. In *The Lonely American: Drifting Apart in the Twenty-first Century*, psychiatrists Jacqueline Olds and Richard Schwartz describe how hard it is for people to admit their loneliness. The myth of the self-reliant, independent person is a pervasive American story. The authors devote a full chapter to discussing Americans' living arrangements and with great concern note the growing trend toward living alone. They discuss how living alone can lead to feeling left out and even to paranoia if not checked. "Simply having a roommate to complain to can make all the difference in the world, restoring perspective and maybe even a sense of humor." [1]

[1]Olds J, Schwartz R. *The Lonely American: Drifting Apart in the Twenty-first Century*. Boston: Beacon Press, 2009; P. 89.

People have very different needs for social connection. One person's solitude is another person's loneliness. "Whatever our own individual sensitivity, our well-being suffers when our particular need for connection has not been met.... Evolution fashioned us not only to feel good when connected, but to feel secure." [2]

Housemates provide human connection. Michelle, married with two children, decided to rent a room because her husband travels often and she wanted to have another person around. She's thrilled with the way her housemate has blended with her family.

Shana says about her housemates, "We notice changes in one another and ask if the other is okay. When that happens, I feel that I don't have to hold the whole world up on my own. It's been such a gift."

Extra Hands

Every home requires ongoing maintenance. From the daily tasks of cleaning dishes to the weekly tasks of trash removal to the seasonal tasks of window washing or shoveling snow, completing these tasks requires energy and time. When there are housemates to share these tasks, everyone has less work to do.

For a person who is limited in what she can do by virtue of age or infirmity, a housemate can mean the difference between being able to stay at home or having to move to a facility with paid assistants. There are programs around the world[3] that work specifically to match seniors and others with housemates for reduced (or no) rent in exchange for regular help around the house. This help can include cooking, shopping, cleaning, or the companionship of eating meals together. The program staff screens candidates, makes matches, and helps the housemates negotiate their contract. Many programs stay in touch with housemates to ensure that the match is satisfactory for both parties.

Other people turn to sharing housing when looking for help with child care. When Lisa started sharing housing, she was interested in having a live-in per-

[2]Cacioppo JT, Patrick W. *Loneliness, Human Nature and the Need for Social Connection*. New York: W. W. Norton
[3]HomeShare International. URL: http://homeshare.org and National Shared Housing Resource Center. Shared Housing: More Than Just a Place to Live. URL: http://www.nationalsharedhousing.org.

son who would occasionally be able to baby-sit her two children. She offered reduced rent for this help. She has liked having housemates so much that she has kept doing it long after her children have left home.

Whatever arrangement you have, it is essential to be clear about this when advertising and interviewing potential housemates. Chapter 12, "Daily Living, Sharing the Home" helps you think about this issue.

Living Light

Those who share housing have less of an impact on the planet than if they were all in separate dwellings—each person's "carbon footprint" is smaller. Sharing housing also allows for sharing furniture, appliances, kitchen utensils, and tools. Each person needs less stuff.

Making Changes

Many people have a hard time thinking about sharing housing. The idea of making a change in the way they live is difficult and easily rejected. When householders consider sharing housing, a whole range of objections quickly surface. "I can't imagine living with a stranger." "I don't want to lose my privacy." "I'm too sloppy." "I'm too neat." "I don't like loud music." "I'm too set in my ways." "What if it doesn't work out?" "No one could live with me."

If you are considering sharing housing and are hesitant, then the best thing to do is to read this book through. Once you understand the process of finding and keeping good housemates, you will see that you can manage most of the particular concerns about sharing housing that you have. Use the worksheet at the end of this introduction to list both your concerns and what you want in a home sharing arrangement. The exercise of writing will help you find answers as you read.

Says Kirby Dunn, Director of HomeShare Vermont, "We've done the surveys. People say they're happier, sleeping and eating better and feeling safer in their homes with someone around. If I sold you that as a drug, you'd pay thousands.[4]"

[4]Leland J. "Homes at Risk, More Owners Consider Taking in Boarders." New York Times, July 16, 2008. URL: http://www.nytimes.com/2008/07/16/us/16share.html.

Worksheet

Before reading through this book, it might be useful to list your beliefs, hopes, and fears about sharing housing

What I want ...	What I'm worried about ...

Section 1 *Getting Ready*

Chapter 1

Initial Decisions - The Householder

Sharon, a television producer with a large house in the suburbs of New York, got laid off and found herself struggling to make ends meet. It was an unfamiliar experience for her. "I never had money problems before," she says. But now she was having money problems, and her expenses were decidedly higher than her income. Her decision to rent a room in her house was not an easy one, but the more she thought about it, the more sense it made. She had a big house with an extra room, and the rental income would help her meet her expenses.

In thinking about renting out a room, Sharon, like every householder, had to make two different decisions: which room to rent, and how much to charge.

The Room

In choosing which room will go to the housemate, the two most important considerations are access to a bathroom and access to the entrance. The easier it is to use both without disturbing other activities in the house, the more attractive and livable your home will be for the future housemate. In some dwellings, the space to rent is obvious. Melanie rented a room in a basement that was adjacent to the family room, with its own bathroom. She says, "Most of the time I had the entire area to myself. It worked out pretty well." Sometimes, a house is built so that a housemate can have an entire floor. When Diane moved into her friend's very large house, she took over the front portion of the second floor. They worked it out so that she had her own apartment with a hot plate and a small refrigerator. She also used the house kitchen.

Is the room furnished or unfurnished? If you have furniture in the room and you don't mind it being used, offer the room furnished. But don't leave your Aunt Sally's heirloom antique desk in the room if you aren't willing to see it with scratches on it. Accidents happen, and other people may not be as careful with your things as you are. This is reality. The same thing is true for sharing linens and towels. If you like things "just so," don't share your belongings with the new housemate.

You must move out of the room completely. Once your housemate has moved in, you should have no reason to go into the room. Each person should have her own space that is hers alone and to which she can retreat without being disturbed. This is an essential part of sharing housing: You give up the room in exchange for rent.

The Rent

The next thing to decide is how much to charge for the room. You can't ask for more than the market rate, so do some research. Track your findings in the worksheet at the end of this chapter. Look at the ads in your area for shared housing, which will give you a good idea of the range of rents being charged in your area. Look for ads for places that are comparable to what you are offering. Then ask yourself where your room fits into this range. Are you offering amenities that put your room at the top of the range? Or are there drawbacks about the room and/or space that put a fair rent at the bottom of the price range?

Don't get greedy. You want your future housemate to feel that he is getting a good deal. Bad things can happen if you charge too much. For example, you might not be able to rent the room, and it just sits there empty. But even worse is having someone agree to the rate, move in, and then start feeling that he is paying too much. You do not want to live with the housemate's resentment.

If you rent your house, you may want to divide the rent evenly between you and your housemate. This is a common decision. And it's a good one, providing all other things are equal. But if one bedroom is huge and sunlit, with a walk-in closet, and the other is dark and small with no closet, the two rooms are not the same and the housemates should not be paying the same rent.

There are various methods for figuring out how much each person should pay. Some do it mathematically, by figuring out the sizes of the rooms and the portion of the total rent each room represents. Others do it by eye and feel. This is up to you. The main point is that everyone living in the home should feel that he or she is getting a fair deal.

Utilities and Other Costs

The costs of heating, air conditioning, electricity, water, cable TV/Internet, etc., are either extra costs or are included in the rent. Which is better? It depends on you. If you include the utilities in the rent, you will save yourself a tremendous amount of time working on bills and figuring out who owes what. You also save yourself the potential aggravation of housemates requesting that they not pay for utilities when they are absent for periods of time. The first year that Phillip and Jillaine shared their house, they split the bills evenly with their housemate. They found this to be time consuming and frustrating. After that first year, Phillip and Jillaine chose to simply include utilities in the rent.

Another question is whether you will share a telephone. These days, so many people use only their cell phones that this may not be a concern. However, if there is a house telephone, you should decide whether you will share it or ask your housemate to make her own arrangements for a telephone.

If you choose to include utilities in the rent, make sure you figure out the average cost for each utility over the course of a full year. This is important because the use of heat, air conditioning, and electricity can fluctuate a lot with the change of seasons. If you are worried that utility charges might change—for instance, because of a large spike in the price of oil—you might make an agreement early on that all housemates will chip in to cover the higher costs.

The other choice—dividing utilities and paying each month—has the benefit of making each person more responsible for his use of electricity, heat, and air conditioning. In the house Ann lived in, each person had one bill in his name and took responsibility for paying for it and collecting from his housemates. In that way, the work was evenly distributed. However, if you are the householder, all the bills will be in your name, so you should maintain control over them to make sure that they get paid. There is software available for sorting out the bills that can simplify the task of month-end accounting, for instance The Housemate's Companion (http://www.housematescompanion.com). A simple spreadsheet can also be used.

Consider whether you have other regular housing costs. For instance, you might pay for trash removal, snow plowing, or a lawn service. Some householders don't charge their housemates for these services, others do. It is up to you to consider whether or not to include them.

Deposits: Security and Rent

You should always ask for and receive, at minimum, a security deposit. For some it is standard practice to ask for the first month's rent, the last month's rent, and a security deposit that is as much as a month's rent or half of that. Yes, it is a lot of money to ask of the housemate, but this is the money that protects you against her leaving in the middle of the night after not having cleaned her bathroom for a year. With a security deposit, you can hire a cleaner, and with the last month's rent, you have time to find a new housemate. Do not be afraid to ask for this money. You have a right to it. You are taking the risk of sharing your home. The deposit is a clear statement from your future housemate that she is worth the risk. If a potential housemate doesn't have the resources to meet this requirement, can you afford to have this person as a housemate?

By the way, when you receive that money, put it in a savings account. In some states, it is the law that you must do so. Check with your local housing board to determine the requirements in your state (see "Resources" at the end of this book). Keep that money separate from your spending so that you have it to cover the last month's rent and can return the security deposit to the housemate who is leaving everything perfect.

Those are the key decisions: the room, and the money—rent, utilities and deposits. Use the worksheet on the next page to record your decisions.

The Next Step: What Do You Want in a Housemate?

You might think you are ready to write the ad or posting. Not so fast. You want a good housemate, right? You want a housemate who can live in your space comfortably with you. Before you write the ad, think through your requirements for a housemate. You can skip to Chapter 4, "How Do You Want to Live?" which discusses this critical step. Or you can read Chapter 3, "Initial Decisions—The Home Seeker." This chapter describes the decisions the home seeker should make before starting to look for housing.

Worksheet

Record your decisions about renting a room in your home

Room

What does the room offer the future housemate? (Check those that apply.)

[ ] Private entrance   [ ] Easy access to entrance
[ ] Shared bathroom   [ ] Private bathroom
[ ] Furnished   [ ] Unfurnished
[ ] Other: _____

Rent

Price range found in local postings   _____

My monthly housing cost (rent or mortgage)   _____

Utilities

For all utility bills, add up an actual year's worth of bills and divide by 12. This will ensure that you don't underestimate the yearly cycle of heat, air conditioning, and electricity use.

Average per Month
Heat   _____
Electricity   _____
Gas   _____
Water   _____
Cable   _____
Internet (might be combined with cable)   _____
Telephone (if shared)   _____

Do you have other maintenance expenses, such as lawn service, snow removal, or trash pickup? Would you expect your housemate to help pay for them?

Other   _____   (average per month)

Total monthly utility cost   _____
Percent charged to housemate   _____
Total housemate cost for utilities per month   _____

Amount you will charge a housemate   _____   (rent plus utilities, if applicable)

All worksheets can be downloaded at www.sharinghousing.com

Chapter 2

Initial Decisions - The Home Seeker

When looking for housing, the logical place to begin the process is to figure out how much you can spend on housing and where you want to live. After those two basic decisions are made, you can think about your requirements for the physical space. This chapter discusses the physical space considerations. The next chapter discusses the housemate arrangement. There is a worksheet at the end of this chapter to record your decisions.

How Much Can You Afford?

First, think about your take-home pay after taxes and other deductions. It used to be that the budgeting standard was that you should spend 27 percent on housing, including utilities. This is about one week's pay. As housing has become more expensive, however, this figure has crept up to 30 percent or more. Budget experts also state that on average, 15 percent of a car owner's income is spent on transportation: car payments, maintenance, gas, etc., and that food is also 15 percent of income. Use these guidelines to determine how much you can afford to pay for housing. Once you know how much you can afford, you can start to think about where you want to live.

Where Do You Want To Be?

Do you want to live near where you live now, or in another area? Are you looking in the area where you have been living? If so, you probably already have a good sense of the neighborhoods and prices. Are you relocating? Then you will need to learn about the new area and the costs of housing.

You should think about your transportation to and from your work, school, and other regular activities, including your visits with family and friends. Think carefully about how your location will affect your commute to your regular activities. Consider the costs in both time and money. John chose a location in the middle of the triangle formed by his main activities: work and folk dance events. Everything was the same distance. This location also gave him a reverse commute—he was going in the opposite direction from most of the traffic.

Look at not only miles but also time. In the Washington, D.C. area, for instance, crossing the Potomac River to get to work can easily add two hours a day to your driving commute. Test the commute at commuting time. Mary Beth lived in a lovely suburban section of Maryland, next to Andrews Air Force Base. Since everyone on the base started and ended work at the same time every morning and evening, at these times the road in front of her house turned into a traffic jam. If she didn't leave early enough, it could take her an extra hour to get to work. The rest of the time the road had very light traffic.

The more time you spend in a car driving, the more it will cost you. Use the Federal rate for car mileage to calculate the cost of different regions. The Federal rate includes gas and the wear and tear on your vehicle. (Look this up at www. gsa.gov/mileage—the rate changes periodically. Sometimes it changes during the year, if gas prices spike or drop.) Also consider parking costs, if applicable.

If your area has public transportation, look into how useful it will be for you. Can you use public transportation to commute to work? Housing located close to public transportation is always more expensive, but it's possible that using public transportation would save in car costs and end up being the better option.

Your commute is your first consideration. Other aspects of your location to think about include access to amenities such as parks, stores, restaurants, entertainment, and proximity to friends and family.

The Physical Space

What kind of physical space do you want to live in? Housing styles vary across regions and within an area: triple-deckers in Boston, high-rise apartments in New York and Chicago, single-family ranches in Seattle, adobe houses in Phoenix, new condo developments everywhere. What is available to you depends on where you live. Do you have strong preferences or dislikes? If you do, that will help you narrow down your options and focus your search for a home.

Can't Live With/Without

A useful way to think about physical space requirements is to consider what you can't live with and what you can't live without. If there are aspects of your physical requirements that are non-negotiable for you, then you can easily eliminate housing that doesn't meet your requirements, making your housing search easier. You won't waste your time considering spaces that don't meet your essential criteria. However, be careful about this list—don't make up "must-haves" just to have a list. You don't want to limit your choices un-necessarily.

Here are some categories to consider. These reminders will help you to be aware of considerations that might be overlooked. Also, you may have your own uncommon requirements for your physical space. Read this list and then create your own lists of "what I can't live with" and "what I can't live without." Use the worksheet at the end of this chapter to capture your thoughts.

Safety

What does "safe" mean to you? For many people, safe means that one can walk and/or drive in the neighborhood without fear. One way to learn about a neighborhood is to ask the local police. Call the station and talk to the person who answers the phone.

Access to Public Transportation

Is public transportation essential? Or useful? If so, how far are you willing to walk to the bus or train? How often does the bus or train need to run? Are weekdays only okay? Or do you want access on weekends late at night?

Parking

If you have a car, what kind of parking must you have? Off-street? Garage?

The Natural Environment

Do you have a requirement for trees, parks, and/or a country setting?

Light

How much light do you need? Can you live in a room that doesn't get much light? Or must you have sun streaming in all the time? Are you likely to be home only when it is dark out? Do you need to have sun in the morning to get you up?

External Noise

Street noises, children crying, dogs barking, machines running, neighbors—all these can cause noise. Some people are very sensitive to any kind of noise and can't sleep in an apartment on a busy avenue. Some people can live in apartments that are eye level with elevated trains that go by every 10 minutes. Some people need silence to be able to concentrate on their activities. What do you need or want concerning noise? What can't you live with?

Outside Space

Do you need outdoor space? What kind? For what purposes? Do you have to have a yard, a garden, or a deck or porch?

Private Bathroom

Do you need to have your own bathroom? Would sharing a bathroom be okay, or is it out of the question?

Appliances

Do you require a washer and dryer? A dishwasher? A microwave? Broadband Access, Cell Phone Coverage, Cable TV?

Though broadband access and cell phone coverage in cities has become commonplace, there are rural locations where broadband and cell coverage are not available. If broadband and cell phone coverage are essential to you, make sure they are on your list. If cable TV is essential, put it on the list.

Furniture/Storage

What requirements do you have for your things? Do you have enough furniture to equip an apartment alone, or do you have nothing? Do you need space for storage?

Pets

For pet owners, this is the first requirement. If you have a pet, you need to live where that animal is welcome. It won't do to convince someone to take on your pet as a housemate. The first time the pet misbehaves—which will be in your absence—your housemates will be reminded that they grudgingly agreed to have the pet in the house. The second and third times, there will be tension, and soon you and your pet will need to find another place to live.

Thinking Ahead

It's possible that you don't have any special physical requirements for your home, but this is unlikely. Thinking ahead can save you time and trouble.

Many home seekers do no more planning than: cost, location, and specific requirements for the physical space. That's fine if you are going to live alone, but if you are going to share housing, you need to think also about your requirements for living in the space. Those are quite different requirements. Chapter 4, "How Do You Want to Live?" guides you through thinking about sharing the home with others.

Worksheet

Record your decisions about the physical space you want to live in

Amount I can spend on housing: _____ (range)

Location(s) I will consider:

_____

_____

_____

Can't Live With	Can't Live Without

Chapter 3

How Do You Want to Live?

To find a good housemate, you need to be able to talk about what you must have and would like to have in a housemate arrangement. This clarity about who you are and what you are looking for will help immensely. Starting to look at postings and advertisements without knowing what you are looking for is like going into a supermarket with no idea of what you need to buy. You'll waste an enormous amount of time and energy considering situations that aren't suited to you. The same is true if you are the householder. Instead of stating your requirements over and over on the telephone to each ad respondent, simply put them in the ad.

In your quest for a good house-sharing arrangement, you need to know what you "must have" versus what you "would like to have." This is a very important distinction. "Must" means that if the potential home or housemate doesn't have it, there's no way the space will work for you. End of story. Walk away. "Must" is your friend; it helps you rule out what won't work for you, simplifying your search and saving you time and energy.

Many people learn of their "must haves" by discovery, that is, they have a housing experience that lacks something they want—but they didn't realize it ahead of time.

Chelsea, a graduate student, moved into a house owned by an older couple who rented out the three bedrooms that had belonged to their now-grown children. The couple was friendly, warm, and welcoming. They were happy to share their kitchen and all the cooking equipment and cutlery. But they did not share the living room. As time went on, Chelsea realized that because there was no space conducive to hanging out, there was no social interaction between housemates. Each housemate lived in his or her room. No one invited friends over. Chelsea found that she wanted a way to informally hang out with others when she was home. In fact, this desire became a "must have" and prompted her to look for a new place to live.

Michelle, married with children, decided to rent a room in her and her husband's house. The first housemate always had her door shut. Michelle discovered that this made her uncomfortable, so when the next housemate moved in, she asked the new housemate to leave her door open when she wasn't at home. She says, "Now the room is part of our home."

Meg thought she'd be fine living on the edge of town, but after a winter of missed buses and standing in the cold, she realized that she had to live closer to reliable public transportation.

Only you can figure out exactly what you must have and what you would like to have in a living space. It's easy to think that you can adapt to anything. But some adaptations are simply too uncomfortable when you are living with them daily. It's really no fun to find yourself unhappy at home because you overlooked or ignored something in a situation that is really not right for you.

Your way of living is unique to you, so figuring out what you need and want in a housemate is worth the effort. Your future happiness is at stake. As you think about this, you will also clarify what it is that you bring to the housemate relationship.

Collect your thoughts in the worksheet at the end of this chapter. You might ask someone who knows you well to help you complete the worksheet.

By all means, be honest with yourself. This is not the time to wish you were different.

Categories to Consider

Gender, Age, Sexual Orientation, and Cultural Preferences

Many people assume they should have housemates who are more or less like them in age, gender, culture, and sexual orientation. However, many other combinations work very well—for instance, middle-aged, single empty-nesters living with young professionals; couples renting to foreign students; seniors with middle-aged adults; mature housemates of opposite sexes. It could be that age, gender, sexual orientation, and cultural preferences don't matter at all. You know what your preferences are.

> Sarah grew up in the Midwest and moved to New York City to try to break into journalism. She was having a hard time finding a place to live when a friend suggested that she look on a website for Jewish life in New York. She found an ad for a room in a Hasidic neighborhood with an unmarried Orthodox woman in her mid-30s. Sarah moved in. She got along wonderfully with her housemate, and they had long talks about religion, American culture, and boys. She says, "It was fascinating." Sarah was invited to Shabbat and learned to keep kosher. For Sarah, living in that neighborhood was like being in a foreign country. She feels that she has traveled far without leaving New York.

> Harold was married for 35 years when his wife died. His children wanted him to move out of the house into an apartment, but Harold really didn't want to leave his home. One day, as he was playing cards at the senior center, a friend mentioned that the adult daughter of another friend was looking for a place to live in the neighborhood. Harold knew the young woman a bit. He decided to offer her a room for a modest sum. After she moved in, they evolved a pattern of eating together many nights of the week, since she is home every evening and likes to cook.

Pets

Dogs, cats, gerbils, snakes, birds, fish: there are all sorts of pets. If you have a pet, then you must have a home that will accept the pet. On the other side, what kinds of pets are you willing to live with? If you are allergic to dogs or cats, this information will be on your "can't live with" list. If you are afraid of dogs, you don't want to live with one; put dogs on your "can't live with" list.

> Before I knew better, I convinced a young woman who was unsure about living with my dog to come over and look at the space. I thought my dog was the sweetest, nicest dog. She was hesitant. When she arrived, the dog turned into a monster, barking, lunging, and snapping at her. It turned out my dog sensed the fear in the woman. Fortunately for me, most people like dogs—but I learned then to respect potential housemates' "can't live withs" and not pursue them.

You may love pets, even if you don't have your own. If you like having a dog in the house or a cat to talk to, put this information on your "would like to have" list. One benefit of sharing housing is having pets around even when having your own is not feasible.

Cleanliness

It's an unavoidable fact of life that unless we pick up the sponge, mop the floor, and vacuum the rugs, a dwelling will get dirty. This is one area where housemates really have to see eye to eye in order to maintain the space all want to live in. What do you like? What can you tolerate? What will you maintain?

Deborah and Tim had different tolerances for cleanliness. As a result, they agreed to split the cost of a cleaning person.

Neatness

Closely related, but not the same, is the issue of neatness. A space that isn't neat is cluttered. Clutter comes in all forms, from old newspapers and mail left on surfaces to a piece of clothing left where it was taken off. Again, what do you like, what can't you live with? What can you maintain?

Television

In the average American household, the television is on for more than four hours a day. Many households have a television in every room in the house. Some don't have a television at all. What are your habits concerning television? What are your preferences for what you watch and when? What you can live with in terms of having a television on in the kitchen, living room, and other common areas? For Mike, his large HDTV in the family room has been an asset. It is where he and his housemates congregate to watch sports and hang out with each other. What "must you have" concerning television and what would you "like to have" in your living space?

Radio/Music

What are your habits, likes, and dislikes concerning listening to the radio and/or music? What you do in your own room is your business—assuming that the sound doesn't carry out of the room. Housemates with extremely different tastes can be compatible, providing that what happens in the common areas is agreeable. You may have a desire to listen to music or news when in the kitchen or in other common rooms. What type of music? What kind of news? Do you dislike a particular genre? Are you able to listen to anything?

Alcohol Consumption and Drug Use

Think about your tolerance for drinking and drugs. If you are a non-drinker, moving into a home of heavy drinkers is not going to be a happy arrangement. If you like to use recreational drugs, you shouldn't move into a home that says "no drugs."

Cigarettes

For smokers, cigarette smoking is often the first consideration. Non-smokers don't want to live with smokers. Smokers, most likely, don't want to live with non-smokers. If you smoke, don't tell yourself that you'll quit if you find the perfect, but non-smoking, situation. That's like buying a shirt that's three sizes too small, promising yourself to lose thirty pounds: it's just not going to happen.

Diet

Diets are so personal that you are not likely to overlook this one, unless you don't have a particular diet but the potential housemate does. If you aren't planning to share food, the diet of your housemate may not make a difference, but then again it might. For instance, if you are a vegetarian, how do you feel about the smell of meat cooking? Can you live with it? Consider also your attitude toward food—can you live with someone who has a completely different diet from you? Can you live with someone who cooks foreign cuisines with interesting smells? Does foreignness attract you or repel you? Maybe you never eat at home and whatever your housemate does makes no difference to you at all.

Meals

Sharing meals adds a level of complexity around the housemate relationship that you may or may not want. Meals require planning, shopping, money, cooking, and time. They can add immeasurably to the housemate relationship and provide the convenience of having someone else cook some of your meals, or they can become a source of conflict. The easiest choice is to keep food and meals separate, but that may not be the right choice for you. This is discussed more thoroughly in "Chapter 11: Daily Living, Sharing the Home."

Sociability

Is home a haven of retreat from the world? Or is it a place for friends to gather? Is your shared dwelling simply a place to sleep and store clothes? You don't have to be in agreement with your housemates on this. One person may simply need a place to sleep and keep clothes, while another may host large dinner parties. This can work very well, provided all are in agreement about how the space is to be used. But if one person needs quiet by 9:30 p.m. and the dinner parties usually end at 11:00, with noisy comings and goings, there will be a conflict. Think about what you want and need around sociability.

> When Anne moved to San Francisco from Boston, she looked for a place to live using craigslist. Since she couldn't afford a trip ahead of time, she did it by e-mail, telephone, and with the help of a friend in Boston. One place was attractive because it was huge and she would have three rooms. She talked to Jim, the householder, by telephone and asked a friend to look at the space. On the phone, Jim said that he wasn't looking for a best friend. After she moved in, she discovered he didn't want anything to do with her at all. He wanted her to be invisible. So Anne would rush home after work to cook, eat, and clean up her dinner so that when Jim came home, she would be done and the kitchen clean. Once in her rooms, she was careful never to make any noise. She moved out six months later. Jim could have prevented having a six-month housemate by being upfront and honest about his "must have." Had he stated up front that he "must have" his solitude, he might have attracted a housemate who also wanted exactly that for himself.

Routines

People with different routines can be fabulous housemates; people with the same routines can be fabulous housemates. How do you live? Are you a morning person or a night person? Think about a typical day. How does it start?

When do you eat? How does it end? How are weekends different from week-days? Which of your routines would affect other people in the house? Is there anything in your daily routines that you "must have" or simply "would like to have"?

Ready for Interviewing

If in reading this chapter you have taken the time to record what you need and want in a living environment, you have a very useful checklist to work with. You know what you must have in a living space, you know what you'd like to have, and you know what you can't live with. You are ready to interview a potential housemate or explore with a householder the feasibility of living in his or her house.

Worksheet

Fill out the table below to summarize what you must have, would like to have, and can't live with in a housemate arrangement

Must have	Would like to have

Can't live with

Section 2 *Finding Good Housemates*

Chapter 4

Finding Each Other

The year was 2001, and I was looking for a housemate. I was expecting to make flyers and list my available room with the large research institutions in the Washington, D.C. region. I thought I'd see what there might be on the Internet. I sat down at my computer and Googled "short-term rent Washington DC." On the very first page was something I had never heard of—a site called "craigslist," where I could post the ad for free. I decided to give it a try. Twenty minutes later, I got a phone call from a home seeker, who became a housemate. After that, I never used anything but craigslist to find new housemates.

The Internet

The Internet is an ideal medium for house-sharing ads. Many services are free, and there is no space limitation. The householder can write as much or as little as she wants. Home seekers can scan ads easily. Most Internet services allow the householder and home seeker to contact each other anonymously. This provides a measure of safety—you can explore the viability of a match without revealing your personal contact information too early.

To date, the largest Internet source for ads is craigslist (www.craigslist.org). Craigslist offers local listings for more than 550 cities in over 50 countries. (Yes, you can look for a room in Vietnam!)

Because it is so well known and used, craigslist does have scammers, unscrupulous landlords, and rental agents who take advantage and make offers that are too good to be true. In big cities, the scammers can spam the listings so that it's hard to see the real ones.

When Jefferson started looking for a place to live in New York City, he felt that it would not be a problem at all, since there were so many good listings. Then he started contacting the ones that were interesting. Many times he simply got no answer, or he would get an answer that the cheap apartment wasn't available but the landlord has another one that was a bit more expensive. Sometimes, he would go and look at the space and it would be completely different from what was advertised. After awhile, he would recognize the false postings being repeated. It was very discouraging.

Another downside is that craigslist postings age very quickly. In a tight housing market, any posting older than a week is probably obsolete. For the householder, this means that your ad will be ignored if it gets old. If you haven't found your housemate within a week, you will need to repost the vacancy. For the home seeker, it means checking into craigslist on a daily basis.

Other Internet services also offer housemate-matching services. The services usually ask the householder and the home seeker each to create a profile, most often by asking a series of questions. Sometimes these responses are used to recommend matches. In all cases, there are two things to consider before signing up for an Internet housemate-matching service. The first is whether the website seems to be current and in use. The second is to carefully read the fine print before you use your credit card. Some websites claim that the introductory period is free but actually start charging the full monthly fee from the beginning. Examine the website's financial terms carefully.

Newspapers

Before the Internet, the classified ad section of the local newspaper was the most common way to find "roommate wanted" ads. Although the newspaper is no longer the primary way to advertise, some papers, especially local and small-town newspapers, might have ads. Various categories are used. Look for "Rooms," "Housemates," and "Houses to Share."

Universities, Research Centers, and Hospitals

Many universities and research centers, and some teaching hospitals, have housing offices designed to help find local housing for their teaching faculty, students, and research fellows. In most cases they accept ads from householders who are offering rooms to rent that are reasonably close to their institution. Usually the institution has a website for home seekers to search. Many of the websites are open to the public. In the Washington, D.C., metropolitan area, for example, the National Institutes of Health posts a local housing list on the Web but doesn't make it easy for you to find. Other institutions require access to their system in order to see listings. A phone call to the housing office of these institutions will give you information about whether and how you can use their services.

Neighborhood Bulletin Boards

Despite the almost universal availability of the Internet, there are locations where the Internet is not the primary way to find a home or housemate. Neighborhood bulletin boards can be good sources. They can be found at:

- Supermarkets, food co-ops, farmer's markets
- Laundromats
- Gas stations
- Gyms, pools, exercise classes
- ATM machines
- Elevators
- Schools
- Community centers
- Libraries
- Places of worship
- Coffee shops, cafes, restaurants

Meet-Ups

In New York City, a service called Roommates Wanted, NYC (http://room-mateswantednyc.com) sponsors regular meetings in a club or bar where people looking for housemates can meet each other. This is an alternative to using the Internet. The service is considering expanding to other cities.

Word of Mouth

Another way for housemates to find each other is through their social networks or colleagues at work. Think of the social networks to which you belong, for instance, clubs, organizations, teams, and associations. Then consider how you can get the word out to the network. This might be by talking to people whom everyone knows, through an e-mail, or making an announcement at a gathering. Word-of-mouth housemates can be absolutely wonderful. You start out with something in common, whether it is an interest in singing, playing ice hockey, or tutoring children. They can also be just sort of "okay" or a total disaster. Do not assume that a friend of your friend will automatically be a good housemate, or that two of your friends will be good housemates for each other just because they are your friends.

Deb met Claudia when they were both invited by a mutual friend for a day of sailing. To Deb, Claudia seemed like a fun person. Claudia was in need of a place to live, having been given two weeks to move out by her current householder. Deb, struck by the injustice of the short notice, offered Claudia a room for what she thought was a temporary arrangement. She did this out of the goodness of her heart. Had she adequately interviewed Claudia, she would have realized that Claudia would not be a good housemate for her. The first indication was that Claudia moved in as if it were a permanent arrangement. She also left her stuff all over the house, set up her TV in the living room (which didn't have one on purpose), didn't pay bills on time, and wouldn't adapt her behavior to make the arrangement satisfactory for Deb. For Deb, it ended up being a nightmare.

Many housemate disasters occur when two friends decide to live together without stopping to think about what it really will be like.

> When Ann and her best friend in school agreed to spend the summer together in Boston, they assumed it would be great. However, tensions quickly developed around how they spent money. Both worked in temporary positions, but Ann got more work than her friend, so she had more money to spend. Conservative in her habits, she would be able to pay her portion of the bills at the end of the month, but her friend would often spend too much on partying and couldn't pay her share. Naturally, that led to friction. They survived the summer, but had they been living together permanently, the situation would have been untenable.

If you are considering becoming a housemate with someone you already know, don't overlook the guidelines in this book. Have an intentional conversation about how you expect to live in your home. Share your expectations and pet peeves. Do this before you move in together, while you are still in the deciding phase. In both the stories told here, had there been an intentional conversation about living together as described in this book, it is probable that neither disaster would have happened. It's much better to find that out ahead of time than after you move in. That way you keep the friendship.

Sometimes, however, it works out perfectly when friends become roommates:

> When Tim got a job in downtown Washington, D.C., he didn't want to make the daily commute from Baltimore, where he owned a row house with his partner. Tim called his old friend, Deb, who he knew had rented out a room in the past. Deb enthusiastically agreed to have Tim move in. They had an initial conversation about expectations and Tim moved in. In part because of the affection between them they have easily overcome the few conflicts they've had. The arrangement has been working beautifully for over two years.

Worksheet

List the different ways you can advertise

Internet

craigslist: your geographical area: _____

Other Internet services you might use: _____

_____

_____

Newspapers

Local newspaper: _____

Rate for an ad: _____

Universities, research centers, and hospitals in your area:

1) Name: _____

Housing Office phone number: _____

Website address: _____

2) Name: _____

Housing Office phone number: _____

Website address: _____

Bulletin Boards

Word of Mouth

Your social networks (clubs, organizations, and groups):

Method for getting the word out:

Chapter 5

Getting the Word Out

You, the householder, are looking for one person, just one. Your ad must attract that person. Your ad should be specific enough to get that person to contact you, and it should screen out less suitable housemates. Many ads try to appeal to too many people. But yours is the reverse type of ad. You don't need hundreds or even tens of responses—you just need a few, one of which is typically the best choice. A good housing ad is focused and specific, like a job posting or a matchmaking ad. The best ad is the one that causes your future housemate to say, "Oh, that one is for me!"

Consider the following ad, reproduced in its entirety:

> $850 + 1/2 utilities. Professional, non-smoking female looking for housemate. The house is very conveniently located near shopping, major commuting routes 495/93, 1.5 miles from commuter rail station in Andover Center, and 0.1 miles from express commuter bus stop to Boston. No smoking. Two rooms available for your private use (i.e., bedroom + office/sitting room/guest room) (rooms can be furnished if requested). Hardwood floors throughout. Large, well-outfitted kitchen, large living room with fireplace, dining room, two full bathrooms, yard, washer/dryer and exercise equipment in basement, driveway. Cable and high-speed Internet ready. North of Boston, near Lawrence, Methuen, Tewksbury, North Reading, North Andover, Haverhill, Lowell, Haverhill at North Main St.

It sounds like a lovely space. The ad contains a great deal of detail about what's in the house. But it says nothing at all about what the householder is looking for in a housemate and nothing about who is living there. There is no indication of how the space is used, what the current resident is like, and what she wants in a housemate, other than a non-smoker.

Six Parts to a Good Ad

The ad you write needs to have six types of information:

1. Location
2. Features of the room and house
3. Something about the personality of the household
4. Something about whom you are looking for
5. Costs and references
6. Contact information

Location

The location of the place to rent is stated in the subject line or headline of a paper ad and specifies the larger geographical area with a name that is commonly known. The headline should also describe a feature that would catch the eye, e.g., "close to public transportation," "lovely Victorian," or "large yard for gardening."

Features of the Room and House

The first few lines of the ad should describe the features of the room or space, its attractive qualities, and its size. Be honest about the space, but at the same time present it in its most attractive light. I used to rent out a tiny room that had two windows. This became "sunny, cozy, small room." My description both told the truth and put a positive spin on it. I had people see the room and decide that it was too small for them, but I also had people look at it and decide that they liked it.

Potential housemates will want to know the basics—the size of the room, bathroom access, and how much light the room gets. Anything else that makes the room special should be described. A room that gets no sun and is dark all day might be just right for someone who works the night shift and sleeps all day. You are looking for a person who is going to be happy and satisfied as a housemate, so be honest and clear.

For the features of the house, home seekers generally want to know about access to parking and/or public transportation, the size and use of common rooms such as eat-in kitchens and living rooms, and media availability. In addition, if the home has another attractive feature that you're planning to share, such as a yard or a pool table, be sure to include it. Be descriptive in picking out the most important features that will affect the home seeker's experience.

Personality of the Home

The next few lines of the ad should describe the current occupant(s) and how the home is used. It's a good idea to start with the number of housemates and their genders and age range. Next, describe the energy and feel of the home. Is it active, with people coming and going, or is it quiet? Do the current residents have regular work schedules, or are they students or have some other unusual schedule? Does anyone stay home all day? Are there residents who travel a good deal?

If there is a common theme for the residents, this is the place to say so. Perhaps everyone is interested in sports, or loves to play video games, or is engaged in social action. Maybe there is no common theme and the residents live their own lives. Some home seekers want a house in which each person is independent. If there are animals in the house, say so. There's no point in talking at length with someone who is allergic to cats if there is one in the house.

Whom You Are Looking For

Next, describe what you want in a housemate. This is the part of the ad that a home seeker reads and says, "Oh, that's the right place for me." For years, I was able to find just the right person by putting "no TV" in the ad —there was none in the house, and I didn't want one around. Usually fewer than 10 people would express interest in the space, and one of them would become a housemate.

You cannot write an ad that discriminates on the basis of race, color, national origin, religion, sex, familial status (married, divorced, single, parent, etc.) or disability or handicap. This is a Federal law and it covers housemate ads. The law generally prohibits stating, in any notice or ad for the sale or rental of a dwelling, a discriminatory preference in any of those protected categories. You can't specify a preference in any of these categories in your ad. You can't say you are looking for a "female" or "Christian" or "Vietnamese" person. You can describe *yourself*, e.g., "I am a Christian male." If there is a shared kitchen or bathroom, you can state a preference for the sex of the housemate. It is your choice whom you invite to share your home, so you can sort out your preferences in the interview process rather than in the ad.

Costs and References

List all the costs associated with the living situation. Specify the rent, utilities, and any deposits required. Make it all transparent. You want to talk with people who can meet the basic financial costs of renting a room in your house.

You will want to have references for anyone who is to move into your house. Say so in the ad so that the home seeker is not surprised when you ask for them.

Contact Information

The last part of the ad is your contact information. Most people prefer not to use their names or their personal e-mail addresses. Many Internet services automatically give you an anonymous e-mail address. If you prefer to post the ad elsewhere, you can create a free e-mail account (through Google, Yahoo, Hotmail, etc.) for the specific purpose of receiving responses to your ad. Or you may be perfectly comfortable giving out a phone number for inquiries. Either way is fine—it's a matter of what you're comfortable with. Keep in mind, though, that an anonymous e-mail contact means that the home seeker has no way to reach you if you turn him down, which could be an advantage. A telephone contact, in contrast, is immediately personal and you can start the interview process right away.

After you have written the first draft of your posting, ask friends to critique it. Hone it carefully. Remember, you aren't looking for just anybody to fill the space in your house or apartment. You are looking for the person who will be a good housemate for you. You do not need to be brief, since there are no limits to the length of an ad on the Internet, but as with any good marketing effort, you need to be clear and accurate.

Model Ad

Here is an ad for a housemate situation that meets all the criteria described.

> Brattleboro. In town. Walk everywhere. Large fenced area with big garden. 9' by 12' second-floor room, unfurnished. Sunny. Shared bathroom and kitchen. Wireless Internet, no TV. We are two women with three dogs and one cat. Interests: organic gardening, holistic health, and alternative ways to earn a living. We are looking for a good fit. You will have healthy habits and like living with pets. No smokers. Meals are independent. No additional pets, please. $500/month. First and last month's rent + $250 security deposit, references required. Contact:
>
> _____

When you write an ad that is targeted and descriptive of what you are looking for and what you are offering, half the effort is done. As Madeleine said after she had written a very specific and clear ad: "I'm not worried now, I've relaxed. I'm sure that the right person will show up."

Exercise

The ads below are real ads from craigslist from one city on the same day. They are reproduced as they were posted, including misspellings. Read the ads and consider how well each of them contains the six types of information described in this chapter. The six types are: location, features of the room and house, the personality of the home, whom you are looking for, costs, and contact information.

> 1. $600 Share Home With ONE Person (Methuen)
> I'm a 54-year-old gay man in Methuen. I have a beautiful 7-room, 2-bedroom home with a room for rent. I'm a non-smoker/drinker/ drugs. The house is furnished and the room has cable. The rent includes utilities. This is a great deal for a guy who needs a QUIET and STABLE home while in transition. Please give me a call to set up a time to see the house... Thanks! [Contact info: phone number/ name]

What, if anything, is missing?

Answer: The householder describes the house, a bit about himself, and what he is looking for in a housemate. He doesn't describe the room to be rented or the facilities. He doesn't say anything about the location, nor does he describe the financial conditions for moving in. He doesn't ask for references.

> 2. $450 Roommate Wanted ~ Great Apartment (Lowell, Route 38)
> I am a female professional environmental scientist and an artist that is looking for someone that is reasonably clean, respectful, and responsible, mid 20's 30's, non-smoker or occasionally smokes outside. I am a pretty laid back, fun, open minded individual and I tend to keep my home life fairly quiet. I am looking for one roommate to share a 2-bedroom/1-bath apartment in the Belvidere area of Lowell. This is a beautiful apartment with hardwood floors, tin ceilings, and

a lot of character. The apartment is relatively large and is located on the first floor of a multi-unit house. Neighbors are all young professionals. There is off street parking and a separate garage for some storage. The available bedroom is mid-sized (7x12). There is a large fully furnished living room and kitchen for shared common areas. There is also a three season porch that is opened up in the warmer months. There are coin-op laundry facilities in the basement and I have wireless internet. Great location....minutes from downtown Lowell, UMass, 495 and Rte. 3. Right near 133/38/110. No additional pets, as I already have two indoor Maine coon-cats. They are very friendly and playful. Rent is $450/month plus utilities. Hot water is included in rent. Shared utilities outside of rent will include electric and gas (heat). Utilities will average $150-$175 in the winter months and be less in the summer months. First and security deposit in advance. You will need to fill out an application and sign a lease to move in. Please call me if you are interested – [telephone number]

What, if anything, is missing?

Answer: This householder has given home seekers a good sense of her, the apartment, and the neighborhood. The good features of the apartment are described, as well as the two Maine coon cats. One thing the ad is missing is a unique description of what the householder wants in a housemate. "Clean, respectful, and responsible" are clichés. Wouldn't every householder want those qualities? She doesn't ask for references.

3. $475 Roommate needed to share 2 bedroom apartment (Haverhill) Female college student seeks female roommate to share 2-bedroom apartment in Haverhill. Rent is $475 each plus utilities. Looking asap.

What, if anything, is missing?

Answer: Missing from this ad are adequate descriptions of the apartment, the room for rent, the householder, what the householder is looking for, and full financial arrangements. She doesn't ask for references.

4. $610 Available May1 (Somerville) (map)
3 bedroom house hardwood floor 9"x10" $610 rent/utilities included month-to-month pay first and security when moving in. Washer/Dryer are available in the basement included in the rent, internet available, off street parking, 10 minutes to Wellington station (orange line).We welcome foreigners we can always help. Looking for a roommate who is clean, responsible, open-minded, mature, no smoker. We are professionals a female Spanish teacher/Medical Interpreter from Panama (female 40) an Indian Student (male 28) and a Harvard student from France (female 25) she is going back home by the end of April. We are very friendly and respectful. Previously we had people from Hungry, Italy, Germany, Turkey, Cypress, Cuban. If you're interested, please e-mail me and leave the best way to contact you. Reply to: [e-mail address]

What, if anything, is missing?

Answer: This ad has the best description of the household and what they are looking for of all the ads here. The householders also describe themselves. What is missing is some interesting detail about the house and the room for rent. The financial arrangements are clearly stated. They don't ask for references.

5. $575 Near Merrimac, Avail. Now. 4bdrm 2 ba (North Andover) (map)
Across from Merrimack College, Avail Now. 4 bdrm 2 bath -- 1 room available -- 4 bedroom and 2 bath to share with 3 other guys. -- Big Yard and Garage. -- Utilities split 4 ways among tenants. -- No lease, first month and last and security deposit required. -- Current tenants live with 2 dogs. May consider other pets. -- See pictures to appreciate. -- free washer/dryer and lawn/snow care taken care of.

What, if anything, is missing?

Answer: This ad describes the space for rent and the location, but doesn't offer any personal descriptions. It would not cause a reader to say, "that one's for me!" The poster doesn't ask for references.

> 6. $675 Spacious Room in convenient location! (Watertown, MA) (map) Nice clean bedroom in beautiful condo with 3 bedrooms, 2 1/2 bathrooms and balcony in quiet neighborhood. Washer/dryer in unit. Street parking available. No pets. No smoking. NO BROKER FEE. All utilities included (heat, electric, water). Near shops, restaurants and more in Watertown Sq. or along Mt. Auburn St. Perfect location for commuters to downtown Boston, Cambridge or suburbs. Easy driving connections to Storrow Drive, Memorial Drive, Rte 16 and Mass Pike. Buses to Harvard Square, express to downtown and Copley Square. Commuter Rail - Fitchburg Line is accessible.

What, if anything, is missing?

Answer: This is a nice description of the convenience of the location. However, no information is given about the character of the house or the room that is for rent. The householder also gives no information about himself (herself?) or the type of house that it is. The details on the financials are also missing. References are not requested.

Chapter 6

Contact and Interviews

The key to finding a good housemate is your screening and interview process. Do this part carefully and completely, and you will find a good housemate. Do it badly and you can end up in a situation that is mediocre or worse. This is true for both the householder and the home seeker.

The screening process has three phases, and in each phase you learn more about whether the potential housemate fits your requirements:

1. The first contact by e-mail or telephone
2. A telephone interview
3. The in-person meeting

First Contact

Since e-mail and the telephone require a lot less effort, your goal should be to meet in person only those prospects who have passed the "must have" and "can't live with" criteria. Both householder and home seeker should be clear on what their basic requirements are. If you haven't done that thinking, go back to the Chapter 3, "How Do You Want to Live?" and do it!

The home seeker makes the first contact. He sees an ad and responds, either by e-mail or by telephone. An ad posted on the Internet will typically have an e-mail address and might also have a phone number for contacting the house-holder. In responding, the home seeker should write something about why he is interested in this particular ad. What about the ad caught his attention? While it might be simply the location, it is best if there is something specific about the ad that was appealing. In responding, the home seeker should also state his critical "must haves." For instance, if he has a pet or can't walk up stairs, he needs to know right away if the prospective situation can accommodate his needs.

The householder receives this e-mail and reads it. If the home seeker's "must haves" are not a problem, the householder will respond with some of her own "must haves." However, if the home seeker's "must haves" aren't met by the householder and the home, the householder should not continue the interview process. There is no point for either party to continue. This is a key point. Living in a home that doesn't meet your "must haves" is a recipe for unhappiness. If the applicant and the living situation are not a fit, it is polite for the householder to respond with a note saying something like, "Thank you for your interest. However, your requirements are not a match for our home. Good luck with your search." You are not obligated to respond to the home seeker at all, but letting the person know is good manners.

E-mail allows each party to explore the fit anonymously. In the exchange, both householder and home seeker can find out whether their "must have" and "can't live with" conditions are met. But these exchanges shouldn't go on too long. If there are no red flags telling you that this situation won't work, it's time to pick up the telephone. Generally, it is more efficient to get on the phone and talk to each other than to use e-mail or texting. After all, if you are going to be living with the person, you need to get a sense of what she's like. In a real-time conversation, you learn more about the character of the applicants in the way they respond to questions, their tone of voice, the way they use language, and how they engage with you. Make a date by e-mail to have a phone conversation.

At this stage you might research a potential housemate on the Internet. As Mike says, "The way we use social media and networks, you can learn a lot about a person." But also remember that not everything on the Internet is reliable, so check out the information when you talk with the person.

The Telephone Interview

The goal of the telephone interview is to learn enough about the situation and each other to know whether it is worth your time and energy to set up a meeting. For the householder, conducting a telephone conversation retains a level of safety. Up to now, the home seeker does not know the actual address of the home, so if you decide that the home seeker is "not what I'm looking for," you can simply finish the call and wish the home seeker well in finding a place that is a fit. For the home seeker, the telephone conversation can save time. It there isn't a fit, you won't waste time traveling to see the space.

The householder conducts the telephone interview. (In a group home, someone should be the designated telephone interviewer.) A good place to start is to find out why the person is looking for a place to live. There are a number of valid answers to this question. How the question is answered tells the householder a lot about the house seeker, his expectations of housemates, and his current life circumstances. For instance, a home seeker could be moving to the area for a new job or could be leaving a relationship. If he is in a housemate situation, the space may be breaking up due to external forces (the landlord selling the building, for instance), or there may be a problem living with someone in the house. Listen to the answers and probe a bit. You don't need to get the home seeker's life story—just enough to get a sense for whether he is someone you can live with.

The home seeker also should ask why the householder is looking for a housemate. If the previous occupant of the room left because she had problems with the householder, for example, the home seeker should seek to find out what those problems were. How the householder describes the situation will tell the home seeker quite a bit about the householder. The householder should have a reasonable explanation—not one that hides the truth, but one that reflects a lesson learned about the way the householder wants to share her home. The home seeker should ask questions about the new situation until she has a good sense about which of the two parties has the problem. Is the householder difficult to live with? Or was the former housemate difficult to live with?

In this conversation, the householder will want to learn how the home seeker is going to be able to pay the rent and utilities and how steady the home seeker's income is. No householder should risk income on someone who might not be able to pay the rent. Conversely, it is unadvisable for the home seeker to look for a place to live without a reliable income. In the course of the conversation, the householder should also make sure that the person understands the financial arrangement and is prepared to meet it. You don't want to be in the position of inviting someone to move in, only to discover that he can't pay the security deposit. In the same vein, the home seeker might want to know, if the householder is a tenant, what the length of the lease is.

Both householder and home seeker are responsible for ensuring that the potential space meets their basic requirements. This is critically important. Don't assume that, because the posting or ad states a requirement, the home seeker has read it and realized that something in the ad really is a requirement. Occasionally it will happen that a home seeker will respond to an ad despite a clear requirement that she doesn't meet. When my housemate and I were looking for a third housemate, we had an ad that said "no TV." We would start the telephone interview clarifying the "no TV" requirement, and occasionally the home seeker would try to negotiate: "I thought it would be okay if I had it in my bedroom." The trouble with that was that the room for rent was off the kitchen, and TV sound coming out of the bedroom could be easily heard. Our answer was no.

At some point during this conversation, either the householder or the home seeker may realize that the person they are interviewing is not a good fit. Then the interview should end, and no one has invested too much time on exploring a relationship that won't work out. This is not the time to reconsider your "must have" and "can't live with" items. The point of having them is to find a living arrangement that fits you.

How do you turn someone down? You tell him the truth. The truth is that there isn't a good fit. This is no one's fault. You are kind and firm. You wish the person well with his search and get off the telephone. How do you say this? The home seeker might say something like, "Thanks for telling me about the room. I don't think it's a good fit. I hope you find the right housemate." The householder might say, "I really appreciate your interest in the room. I'm sorry, but I don't think it'll work out. Good luck with your search." You want to be firm, fair, and friendly, but you don't need to be specific. If your "must haves" and "can't live withs" have not been met, don't meet the person or go look at the space. You are wasting your time.

If the householder determines during the phone interview that the house-mate relationship is likely to work, then she invites the person to see the space. Up to this time, the home seeker hasn't been told the exact address of the house. This is on purpose. It is protection for the householder. If the applicant is turned down, she can't show up on the doorstep. For the interview, find a time that is convenient for both of you.

Meeting in Person

Householder(s)

When there are several people in the house, it is best if everyone is present for the showing and group interview. Because you have spent time screening potential housemates before showing the space, you will probably not have a lot of candidates at this point. This is good since it makes the process easier on busy households. If you have several candidates and you need to get the household together to meet them, it may be convenient to schedule back-to-back showings. Give each one an hour, and be firm about this. You don't want to have to cut an interview short because the next person has shown up.

The single householder looking for one housemate might benefit from having a friend or family member present when showing the home seeker the space. This person both provides safety and can offer another opinion about the potential housemate. Start by taking the home seeker on a tour. Show him the space that would be his, and then show him the rest of the house. Give him time to take it in.

Answer all questions honestly. Offer information about the room and the household that could be a problem after the home seeker moves in. For instance, I lived in an apartment where the available room was an extension to the apartment and had four outside walls (including the ceiling). It was cold in the winter because there wasn't enough insulation in the walls. Because the home seekers were told about this right up front, they made their decision with full knowledge of this issue. No one who moved into that room ever complained.

Sometimes it happens that you have a good telephone interview and, as soon as you see the potential housemate, you know it won't work. This happened to iishana. In the telephone interview, iishana and the home seeker seemed to "have a rapport," so iishana invited the home seeker to see the house and be interviewed. However, when iishana opened the door she saw a person whose appearance was "severe." iishana says, "instantly I knew I couldn't live with her." Also, though the home seeker had said she was fine with animals, when approached by iishana's small dog, she was clearly not comfortable with him. iishana gave her the house tour, but it was half-hearted. The home seeker also knew it wasn't a fit. They parted with the understanding that they would get in touch if either wanted to move forward.

Home Seeker

When you tour the home, take your time and trust your gut. It could be that as soon as you see the house, the room, the kitchen, or the furnishings, you hate it. That makes the decision easy. Thank the householder for her time and leave. On the other hand, it could be that you love everything about the house. Most likely your reaction will be something in between.

Ask all the questions that occur to you. This is a very important conversation. This is when you explore how you would live in the house together, and if you do end up sharing, those questions and answers will be the backbone of your implicit agreement. This first exchange sets up expectations for both of you for how you will live together. You might have questions about how common rooms are shared, storage space is used, or kitchen equipment is shared (or not). If these were talked about in the telephone interview, confirm what was said.

The Interview

If both parties are still interested after looking at the space, settle down to a mutual conversation about possibly living together. Talk about your patterns, desires, and wants. The point of this conversation is to get to know the other person, with the idea that you might be living together. Since you have already talked about your "must haves" and "can't live withs," now is the time to discuss your likes, preferences, habits, and routines.

In this interview, you must discuss how you would share the home. Good housemates can be very different from each other so long as they agree about how they live under the same roof. You don't have to have the same routines, likes, or preferences. One housemate may be a homebody and never go out, while the other is almost never at home. And that might be a great housemate relationship. However, if the one who goes to bed at 9 p.m. is awakened on a regular basis by a housemate who brings home friends to carry on partying after the bars close, then you have a problem.

You need to discuss these things: bills, the kitchen and cooking, household chores, your expectations about guests, both casual and overnight, pet routines (if pets are part of the household), and the use of common living areas and possessions. Before you interview, read Chapter 11: "Daily Living, Sharing the Home," which discusses these areas of sharing housing in more detail. At the end of Chapter 11 is a worksheet to help you clarify how you want to live and prepare you to interview potential housemates. If pets and/or children are part of the arrangement, read Chapters 8 and 9. You can use the interview notes provided at the end of this chapter to guide the conversation.

The importance of discussing all financial arrangements during the interview can't be over-emphasized. There should be no surprises for anyone once home sharing has started.

If you have a significant other, you should say so in the interview. You should be able to provide a description of how much time you expect to spend with this person in your home. Sometimes a housemate who has a significant other really only needs a place to keep clothes because he actually spends all his time elsewhere. Sometimes a housemate expects his significant other to be in his home often. If that's the case, the potential housemate should meet this person as part of the screening process—maybe not at a first interview, but before making any agreement to live together. This is not an intense interview—it is a gut check. If you have a negative reaction to the significant other, you should probably not live with the potential housemate.

This is the time to voice your expectations and preferences. Don't be shy; this conversation is essential. This is the time to be open and frank, stating honestly how you live and want to live. This is the time to ask every question as it occurs to you. Do not withhold information.

If the home seeker realizes that her possessions won't fit in her bedroom and there isn't a need for them in the common areas, then they will have to be stored. Find out if there is a place you can use. Don't assume that because you've seen a garage, attic, or basement, you can use it. When Madeleine was interviewing John as a possible housemate, he realized he would have to pay for storage because there wasn't enough space in Madeleine's apartment. The extra cost of storage was more than John could support, so they did not become housemates.

> After Deb had a horrific house-mate experience she became more careful. The next time she was looking, she took the interview process seriously. She says, "I asked all these questions. I think because I asked them, when he moved in he understood what I cared about. He was tidy and considerate."

As you are interviewing, you are experiencing the other person, getting to know him. You are talking about the particulars of how you would share housing, and you are getting a "feel" for the person. Trust your gut as well as your head. With your head, you are learning if the particulars of the arrangement will work for you. Either you discover that the arrangement won't work and both parties can disengage, or the conversation establishes your expectations for how you will live together. With your gut, you are feeling the person. If the connection doesn't feel comfortable, don't continue. If it is comfortable and there are no other red flags, then you may be ready to share housing with this person.

Do not make an agreement at this time. If you are interested, you should make some statement about your interest, but the decision should be made after the interview, not during it. Both parties should have a chance to reflect on the conversation. For the householder, if you've had an ally present, you need time to talk to that person about his or her perceptions of the situation. Sometimes it happens that you feel a need to meet with the potential housemate again. That's fine, but do this only if you are seriously interested in the housemate.

An important step is asking for and checking references. This step is described in detail in the next chapter.

Worksheet

These are the common categories that should be discussed in the interview, so that you have clarity and agreement on how you would share housing

Kitchen
(Meal time routines, use of fridge/other food storage, use of cooking equipment, cleanliness, other)

Common Rooms
(Patterns for the use of common rooms, music, radio, noise, etc.)

Bathroom (if shared)
(Regular routines: time of showers, baths, toilet seat up or down, cleanliness expectations)

Household Cleanliness and Chores
(Cleaning routines and supplies, trash, expectations for common rooms)

Guests
(Casual and overnight)

Paying Bills
(When, how)

Pets (if applicable)
(Exercise and food routines, cleanliness)

Chapter 7

Checking References

It is absolutely essential that you ask your future housemate for references. Someone can be charming and lovely in an interview but show a different character once you are around him on a daily basis.

This chapter focuses on references for the householder. Though not common practice, it makes sense for the home seeker to also get a reference for the householder. A good reference is a former housemate, a long-term friend, or a work colleague.

The householder should ask the home seeker for two references with names and telephone numbers. The two types of reference you should seek are (1) income verification and (2) housemate habits. Call the references and talk to them about how the home seeker is to live and/or work with. These conversations are very useful in determining the person's trustworthiness and self-awareness. The home seeker might tell you that he always washes his dishes, but a former housemate will tell the truth. After Alexa interviewed Rose, she said, "I got her references and Googled her name. Got lots of information on her. Checking on references gave me time to weigh the pros and cons." Be wary of a person who claims to have lived in shared housing before but can't give you a reference of someone he or she has lived with.

I learned to check references as a result of a bad experience:

I was a bit desperate to find a housemate to help pay the rent, and a young man came looking who seemed just fine. He said he was going to a particular school and that he needed a place to live because his girlfriend was throwing him out. In the interview, he mentioned that he smoked a little marijuana. That didn't bother me at the time, and I invited him to move in. Over the next several months, it became apparent that he smoked marijuana all day long, a situation that was not okay. He fell behind on his rent. I asked him for it several times. Finally, one day he announced that he was moving out and handed me a check for the money I was owed. I was happy he was leaving, called the bank, and verified that the money was there. However, when I cashed the check the next day, the account had been closed. The only connection I had with this guy was a phone number on one telephone bill. (This was before cell phones.) When I called that number, I discovered that it belonged to the young man's sister. In the ensuing conversation, I learned that my former housemate was a con artist and had taken lots of money from many people. The sister was the only person in the family who would have anything to do with him, and even that connection was tenuous. The sister declared, "You're lucky he didn't take more." A reference check might have prevented the whole situation from developing. While it is possible that the con artist might have arranged false references, that takes work and requires an accomplice. More likely he would have moved on to find a more gullible person.

Reference checking should be done by telephone, not through e-mail. Make the phone call. For some, it is a bit scary to call someone you don't know. If it is scary for you, just take a deep breath and do it anyway.

After you make these calls, keep the references' names and phone numbers. Use the worksheet at the end of this chapter to record the reference conversations.

Verifying Income

For income verification, call the person's place of work and talk to her manager or supervisor. Keep the conversation short. Once you have verified the home seeker's employment, you might ask if there is anything the supervisor knows about the person that it would be helpful for you to know. This is an open-ended question on purpose. Whatever the supervisor tells you will help you make your decision.

If you don't reach the supervisor, leave a voice mail. Be direct and clear. "I'm considering____ as a housemate, and I want to verify that she works for you. I'll call again."

Checking Housemate Habits

The other reference is for finding out what the person is like to live with. Before calling, write down what you plan to ask. When you introduce yourself, explain clearly why you are calling and ask the person for ten minutes of their time. That's enough for you to get the information you need.

Start the conversation by introducing yourself and explaining your purpose. Then, find out how long the referrer has known the home seeker. Next, if you are talking with a former housemate, find out why that relationship ended. Endings tell a great deal about a person. The ending probably had a good reason, since this person has agreed to provide a reference.

Two general questions should lead you into a conversation. Ask, "What did you like most about living with ____?" and "What did you like least about living with ____?" Ask open-ended questions (requiring more than a simple "yes" or "no") that allow the reference to talk and you to listen. If you have any particular concerns, make sure you ask about them. Keep an eye on the clock and end the call at the ten-minute mark as you promised, thanking the reference for their time.

The Invite

The reference checks give you more information with which to make a decision. You can either confidently decide to share housing with the person you checked on, or you can decline. It's up to you.

Assuming the references check out, you are now ready to invite the home seeker to move in. How you make the final contact, by e-mail or telephone, is not important. What is important is the exchange of money. The home seeker needs to give the householder the deposits as agreed in the telephone interview. Nothing is final until money has changed hands. When the home seeker gives the householder all the money required for moving in, the householder gives the new housemate a key. This is a reciprocal exchange. The home seeker has a right to expect a key at this point, so the householder should have one ready to hand over. A date for moving in is established.

Worksheet

Use this worksheet to document your reference checks

Name of home seeker/householder:

Income Verification (for home seeker only)

Name _____

Contact Information: _____
Date of Conversation:_____

Verified? Yes [ ]   No [ ]

Housemate Reference

Name _____
Contact Information: _____
Date of Conversation:_____
Relationship: _____

_____

Years Known: _____

(If former housemate) Reason relationship ended:

What did you like best about living with _____

Why?

What did you like least about living with _____

Why?

Other questions you want to ask:

Chapter 8

Pets

Our pets are part of us, we love them, and when we live in shared housing they become part of the household too.

Dog and cat owners look for homes that welcome their pets—and it is often their first "must have." If you happen to have another sort of pet, one that lives in a cage—bird, fish, gerbil, or snake—this should be mentioned in the telephone interview. What's the point of going to look at a place if the householder absolutely won't have a snake in the house, and you own a little garter snake? Yes, YOU know a garter snake is harmless, but for someone deathly afraid of snakes this won't be a good fit. Imagine starting to move in and as your snake cage comes through the door, your householder freaks out! It is essential that your future housemate agrees to your pets. Being open and direct about your pets will ensure that you find the right housemate for you.

> When Sharon decided to rent a room in her large house she wondered whether anyone would be willing to live with her many dogs. She thought this would make it difficult to find a housemate, so she decided to put that information right up front in her craigslist posting. Anyone living with her would have to tolerate her dogs. She had no problem finding the perfect housemate. When Nikki came for her interview, the first thing she did was greet the two dogs in the kitchen. As Sharon says, "That was very important. The dogs love her."

A dog whom you might live with is one you want to meet ahead of time—in a sense, this is interviewing, but it need not be as intensive as the home seeker interview. Depending on the circumstances, meeting the dog might occur in a follow-up interview or as part of the first interview. In either case, the point of the meeting is to make sure that you can live with the dog. You also want to know that you are comfortable with how your future housemate relates to his dog. Likewise, if you are the dog owner, you want to be sure your future housemate and your dog are okay together.

If you both have dogs, you need to know whether they will get along. Take them on a walk in neutral territory. Watch how they relate. If they ignore each other or play together, this is good. If, on the other hand, they want to fight, you will probably have a difficult time bringing them into one home. They might establish their hierarchy and settle down, but they might not. See how the dogs relate and decide whether they can coexist in the same house.

Daily Routines and Discipline

People can be quite different about how they take care of their pets and the behaviors they allow. The daily routines of pet care revolve around sleep, food, exercise, and elimination. When you share a home, you see up front and close how these daily routines and discipline are manifested. On the positive side, you might learn from each other new and better ways to care for your animal companions. But if your housemate handles her pet (or yours) in a way that you don't like, you should find a different housemate.

In meeting each other's pets, it's the big picture that's important. How much freedom would the pets have in the home? What restrictions would the pets have to live with? Some owners are content to permit dogs on couches, while others are appalled when any animal gets on furniture. Some would like a cat to be in the housemate's room when the housemate isn't home, others are happy to have the cat sit on their laps while working. Some would put dog pads in common rooms, others would restrict a dog bed to the housemate's room. So the question is, what kind of movement is the pet allowed, and is this different when the owner isn't home? Is the cat an indoor or an outdoor cat? Is there a fenced yard for outdoor access? Some hate it when cats get on tables and counters. Others don't care. Some people think dogs belong outside.

Where would a caged pet—a bird, hamster, or reptiles— live? Is it welcome in a common room, or is it expected to reside in the housemate's room? If you and your housemate disagree on this, you will have a problem.

Another interview item for cat owners is the location and care of the kitty litter. Keeping the kitty litter clean is part of owning a cat and is essential when sharing housing. Where will the box be? It must be put where the cat will use it. You don't want the cat deciding to use some other area, like flowerpots. If you live alone, having it in the bathroom might be natural, but if the bathroom is shared, the housemates have to agree to this. If there isn't a good common area, a cat owner should be prepared to have the kitty litter in his room. Keeping caged pets clean and non-odiferous is also essential.

When you move in with your pet, some considerations and adjustments are normal:

> iishana has two dogs and Lisa has one. iishana leaves food out all day and her animals eat when they like. Lisa has a dog who would happily finish off the food in the other dogs' dishes. They decided to have a gate to prevent this.
>
> When Kirsten lived with Sally and Sally's cat, there was often cat hair on the couch in the living room. Kirsten didn't really like the cat hair that ended up on her clothes. They put a cover on the couch for the cat and took it off when Kirsten used the couch.

Discipline can be an area of agreement or one of serious contention. Some people scold, hit, and punish pets who disobey or transgress. Others are so permissive that they have no boundaries for their pets at all. Still other pet owners firmly establish limits and reinforce them with simple corrections. The point is that you should be comfortable with how your housemate takes care of her pet. Likewise, she should be comfortable with how you manage your pet. Observe your potential housemate while interviewing and discuss your approaches to the daily routines and discipline for pets. The worksheet at the end of this chapter can be used to record your routines for your pet so that you can easily describe them when interviewing.

Introducing Pets to Each Other

Introductions are very important. If the introduction between the pets goes badly, it may take a long time for them to recover, and none of the housemates will be happy. Never leave pets in a room together without adult supervision until they have gotten to know one another.

Cats do not like change. When moving into a new home with your cat, keep it in your room for a while with the door closed. If possible, move the cat in last, after all the boxes and furniture have been brought in. Give the cat several days to adjust to the new space.

When a cat is joining a household that already has a cat, the two animals should first be kept separate and given a chance to be curious and get to know each other by sound and smell. Do not assume that the cats will be fine if you throw them together. If they fight when they first meet, they may never get to be friendly. When it seems safe to introduce them because they have each calmed down and relaxed, simply open the door and allow them to approach on their own, each having an escape route for a retreat. How they relate to each other after this will depend on their personalities. Some cats will become best friends, others will ignore each other.

When introducing a cat and a dog to each other, in addition to simply opening the door and making sure that the cat has a way to escape, put the dog on a leash and keep it quiet so the cat can choose whether or not to approach. Once the cat sees the dog settle down, the cat too will relax.

When a new dog is joining a household that already has a dog, do not assume that they "will work it out." Dogs are emotional; a bad start will set the tone for a long time. Start by keeping the new dog in his new room until he has settled there. When you allow the new dog into the rest of the house, watch carefully how the resident dog reacts. The dogs need to establish their relationship. Once they get comfortable with each other, they can relax. There are many good resources on the Web about managing the introductions of dogs in a new home.

Life with Pets

Sharing housing has real advantages for pet owners. Owners can help each other out, feeding the cat while one of them is away on a business trip or vacation, letting the dog out when the owner is late getting home, or taking the dog on an outing just for fun. Mind you, you cannot assume that your housemate will be ready and willing to take any responsibility for your pets. You are the primary caregiver, and you must never forget that.

For some adults, their own lives make it difficult to have a pet, but in a shared housing arrangement they can enjoy living with one.

> When Annabel moved to Boston to pursue a Master's degree, not only did she separate from her husband and leave her children with him, she also left behind her dog of ten years. Though she was excited about her new life, the loss of these daily relationships with her children and dog were wrenching. Though she wasn't actively looking specifically to live with pets, she found a place in which two kittens were resident. For her this was an added benefit.

Pets can add immeasurably to a home. They become a topic of conversation and a source of affection given and received. They become members whose play and personalities are part of the shared housing arrangement.

Worksheet

Use the worksheet below to document your routines for your pet

Name of pet

Routines	Discipline: Allow/Forbid

Name of pet

Routines	Discipline: Allow/Forbid

Chapter 9

Children

Shared housing with children can be a wonderful solution for parents, especially for single parents who are managing everything on their own. There are as many variations as there are types of parents: for example, a nuclear family might rent a room to a single person, two single moms might combine households, or a dad with weekend custody might share with a single person. The type of relationship the adults have with each other and with the various children can range from friendly interest to co-parenting.

Saving money is an obvious benefit of sharing housing. Being able to afford living in a better neighborhood is another benefit. It might also mean access to better schools, libraries, public transportation, and parks. These things are certainly good kids. But maybe even more important is the increased companionship for both children and adults.

Brooke and her child share a house with a friend and his one child. Brooke says, "When we are all together, it makes for a family feeling. The children have camaraderie, and it's not always my job to entertain my child. It's nice to have another adult around. If I have to run to the supermarket for something, I can just go. It doesn't have to be a big deal of packing my son up to take him with me."

Teresa and Jennifer also share a home. Teresa says of the arrangement, "There are so many good things about it. My kids have a better home life and home than I could provide on my own. My housemate's son, who has no siblings, has my kids as friends. They play together. We live in a safe neighborhood in a large house with a yard. The children have a trusted adult to talk to who isn't a parent. I really value this for my teenage son. And I have someone to talk to, too. It will be interesting to see how our friendships develop in the future."

Bruce has his son every other weekend. "Before I started sharing with Sam and his son, I would spend the entire weekend as the entertainer. I always felt that I had to plan special events to keep him amused. Now when he visits, the two play together and we eat meals together. It's a huge improvement."

When children are involved, finding a housemate requires the same sort of careful selection process already described in this book, with some additions.

"Must Haves" and "Can't Live Withs"

When you start thinking about how you want to live, you must consider what you are offering or looking for in the physical space (Chapters 2 and 3). Next, as you consider how you want to live and as you write your list of "must haves" and "can't live withs," include the "must haves" and "can't live withs" of the children. For instance, if your son is allergic to cats, cats are on the "can't live with" list. These "must haves" and "can't live withs" become part of the conversation you have in the telephone interview (Chapter 4).

One resource that exists for single mothers to find each other is CoAbode (www.coabode.org). This is an Internet service specifically for single mothers. After registering, you have access to the database. CoAbode also offers support groups. Some mothers find their housemates through these support groups.

Contacts and Interviews

Chapter 7, "Contact and Interviews," describes two steps for interviewing potential housemates, with the initial interview happening over the telephone. When children are involved, there are at least three steps. If your telephone interview goes well and you are moving forward arrange the initial face-to-face interview without the children present if possible. That way, if it's not going to work out, the children aren't disappointed by possibility and loss.

Introduce the children after you have reached agreement on the essential issues of sharing housing(cleanliness, neatness, meals, noise, chores, and guests), as described in Chapter 12. You might want to get together several times to visit in each other's homes as you explore the idea of living together. You might have meals together or a play date, giving you a chance to learn whether the children are likely to be able to live together. You also get to observe your future housemate relating to her and your children. Although the children don't have to get along right away, you do need to be comfortable with how each adult relates to his own children and to your children.

Parenting

Parenting styles can vary immensely in our society. Some parents are permissive, while others are restrictive. For instance, some parents feel that it is essential for children to have meals and bedtime at the same time every day. Others feed their children whenever the child is hungry and let them go to sleep where they drop. Some parents strictly limit access to screens (television, computer, and video games), while others have no limits. Some believe a child should never be spanked; others feel that spanking is perfectly okay. Some never let their child have sugar, and others keep an ample supply of sugary treats in the pantry.

Children can adapt to different adult requirements, but it is difficult to maintain separate rules when those rules are very different. It's confusing to the children and too easily leads to unhappiness. Children living in the same household don't need to be exactly the same, but the parents should have similar or at least modifiable approaches to discipline and routines.

For instance, while neither Teresa nor Jennifer has a television, Teresa strictly controls video games and Jennifer doesn't. If parents have very different approaches to child rearing, they might learn from each other, but first they need to talk about the topic at length and find out if each of them is willing to adapt to make the situation work. A place to start the conversation is to talk about the routines and discipline you use with your own child. Use the worksheet at the end of this chapter to write down your philosophy of parenting so that you can talk about it clearly with your potential housemate.

When It Works

Parents who share housing are often very thankful that they took the step:

> I never dreamed it would be this amazing. Simpler. Better. Happier. Easier. Cheaper. Most importantly, our boys are having the time of their lives. No more boring weekends watching mom clean the house. No more watching lots of videos or entertaining themselves while she does laundry, pays bills, cooks, etc. Now, when we clean the house, there are two of us sharing the load—taking half the time and getting more done—and meanwhile, the boys are peeing their pants laughing together! It's not been without its transitions, but it's gone amazingly well. And for me, having someone else to talk to, bounce ideas off of, learn from, and share with is incredible. Not to mention that I now can have a bit of a social life, go see a movie, shop at night, go get a coffee...things I didn't do while living alone. And having a built-in baby-sitter that I care about and trust, and whom my son loves, is priceless. My roommate has even started to take classes at night, too, something she wasn't able to do while living alone!

The children in this household feel the same way. There are benefits that can last a lifetime. Says Lori, who lived in a shared housing arrangement in the 1970s and early 1980s: "We girls were only nine months different in age and in the same grade in school. We were often dressed the same and had the same haircuts. People used to question if we were twins (which was so humorous to us). Our six years 'co-aboding,' as you call it, made us family when we really needed it. Now, the two of us 'only children' are not at all alone, but sisters. It has formed us and defined who we are in many ways."

Finding the right housemate when children are involved is a bit more complex than looking just for yourself. Still, it is worth the effort. A good shared housing arrangement can be a joy for all.

Worksheet

Children

*Use the worksheet to document your routines for your children.
Also consider what you allow or forbid in their behavior.*

Routines	Discipline: Allow/Forbid

Section 3 *Keeping Good Housemates*

Chapter 10

Moving In and The First Week

Once you have found your good housemate, you want to keep her. What happens during the first week sets the stage for your continued comfort at home.

The first week is a transition period. Both householder and home seeker will feel a bit vulnerable and a little uncomfortable. This is natural. As Mike says, "I've learned that there is a transition when a new person moves in. It's a bit scary to give someone the key to your house. It's a phase you go through. I'm a bit more cautious around the house, I don't go walking around in my underwear yet." (He has only male housemates.)

On moving day, the householder chooses whether to be helpful or not. Some like to be helpful because it's a nice thing to do, but there is no obligation to do so. If the home seeker is simply renting a room, and "moving in" means putting all his possessions in that room, there is no need for the householder to be present. However, if the home seeker's possessions will be placed in common areas, including the kitchen, the householder should be available for the inevitable questions. It can be very disconcerting to come home and find things moved around! It is much better for the householder to participate in the process and have mutually agreed-upon arrangements for possessions from the beginning.

The first week establishes patterns that become the norm for living together, so this is the time to communicate if something comes up that makes you uncomfortable. It is much easier to mention the thing when it first shows up than it is after the housemate has been doing it for a while. As Mike says, "I can't suddenly make a stipulation that wasn't there at the get-go." This is the week when it's essential to follow the "do it while it's easy" rule. (See Chapter 12, "Guidelines for Happy Households.") This discussion may not feel easy, since this is a new person you don't know very well, but opening up a topic may turn out to be a non-issue.

Here's a story of not dealing with something right away. In order to rent student housing, Mary and her friends needed one more person to qualify. They invited a woman they didn't know very well to join them. When they all moved in, the new woman set up her television in the living room, turned it on, and established herself there. Not knowing how to respond, the rest of the household simply let her do it. It turned out that this housemate watched TV in the living room every day and evening for the entire year. Mary and her friends ceded the living room to the TV watcher and grumbled to each other about it. They should have said something right away. Of course, they also should have interviewed more carefully.

Jillaine and Philip, who chose to share their home with foreigners, say that in the first week, "We tend to treat our new housemates like guests. We are getting to know them and are excited to know them. We often show them around—take them to Great Falls or to a favorite restaurant." Charlene has a completely different approach. She welcomes the new housemate and gives her a tour of the key things that the person needs to know about the house—locking up, using the appliances, where space is for her food, and an orientation to kitchen stuff. She then leaves the housemate to her own unpacking and moving in. She also puts a welcome letter in the room with information about the house and the habits of the residents. (Her letter is reproduced at the end of this chapter.)

In the first few days of living together, have a discussion of "pet peeves." Pet peeves are the little things that individuals dislike that are minor but over time can become an issue. I owe this idea to a housemate of 25 years ago and have used it ever since. Her pet peeve was seeing wet sponges in the sink. Mine is storing plastic containers without their lids.

Householders often write up a list of dos and don'ts that they give to the new housemate upon arrival. This list of specific requirements concerning the care of the home and its appliances can be very useful for all parties. Three examples are included in the worksheet at the end of this chapter. Each has a different tone. These are not offered to suggest that you copy them, but rather to see how differently householders put together instructions for new housemates. Some of the items might be discussed during an interview. The documentation provides a reminder for the new housemate and simply helps everyone know what's going on. If there isn't such a document already created, it can be a good idea for the two new housemates to sit down and put in writing their agreements about how they will live together. This should be done in the first week.

The first week is important. Observe yourself and the patterns you are making in the household during the first week. Make sure that they are comfortable for you. If something isn't comfortable, communicate and adjust. As Kirsten says, "Once you have a routine, it is hard to make changes. So you need to talk about it at the beginning. Once something has been done for a while, it is hard to take it back."

If you followed the interview process described in this book, your new housemate will not be a total stranger when he moves in. You have already established the basics of a good housemate relationship. Now you get to live with your housemate. You may choose to get to know him better. You may share the stories of your day, you may watch movies together, you may have meals together, or you may simply say "good morning" and have a cup of coffee. Now you get to enjoy the spontaneous social exchange that is one of the key benefits of sharing housing. Enjoy having a home that works for you.

Samples of Household Dos and Don'ts

Here are three examples of information given to new housemates when they move in. They each have a particular tone reflecting the personality of the household. Read each and reflect on the type of rules you might create if you are the householder

Example 1 Welcome

Welcome. I thought I'd write down some things that will help you get settled.

Bathroom

The front bathroom is largely yours. Occasionally, [housemate] uses it, and I give the dog a bath there about once a month. To turn on the shower, pull down the ring on the tub faucet.

Kitchen

You have full kitchen privileges. We have a French coffee maker that you can use. (In cabinet below fish tank.) The trash is in the cabinet on the far right side as you face the sink; paper on the right, garbage on the left. The county recycles cans, bottles, and aluminum foil; these go into the blue container on the deck through the pantry door. All trash is picked up on Tuesday morning.

We compost. There is a small container above the sink, which when full goes to the white bucket on the deck through the pantry door. When that gets full I dump it into the compost in the backyard. We run the dishwasher when it gets full.

Our Routines

I'm out of the house by 9:00; [housemate] works at home. [Housemate] is a night owl and sleeps until ten. I'm home around 7:30; we tend to eat dinner around 8. We like to have quiet and privacy during dinner, and we will extend to you the same courtesy.

Other Stuff

There is a washer and dryer in the basement. There is a TV in the living room that receives broadcast stations. You're welcome to watch it and to play videos.

Example 2 Letter of Agreement

We are seeking a housemate who is willing to live in alignment with or at least respect our efforts to live in harmony with nature and with each other:

We are committed to conserving energy wherever possible—not only for financial reasons, but for environmental considerations as well. Therefore, we try to be conscious of our use of water, electricity, and gas (e.g., shorter showers, turning off lights when not in use, being conservative in our use of central heat & air).

We compost much of our vegetable and fruit waste; we also recycle.

We are committed to creating an enjoyable, comfortable, and clean home in which to live. Therefore, while we are neither perfect nor obsessive, we ask that especially in the common areas, each of us cleans up after ourselves, not leaving dirty dishes in the sink, etc. While you are welcome to eat in your room, we have found, living in these older houses, that we must be particularly vigilant about food, open containers, leftovers, etc. in order to eliminate the risk of attracting insects and rodents.

You are responsible for the cleaning of your room and bathroom, and for leaving it in the condition you found it when you complete your time with us. If you experience any malfunctions in plumbing or electricity in your room or bathroom, please alert us and we will have it repaired as quickly as possible. While you are welcome to decorate your room as you would like, please discuss/negotiate with us anything that would alter the condition of the walls, windows or floors, as we are responsible to our landlord for returning the house to the condition in which we found it.

We enjoy cooking and sharing meals, and invite you to participate in this with us if you wish. We are happy to share our food and ask simply for the courtesy of reciprocation.

You are welcome to enjoy the common spaces of the house; we spend most evenings in the living room and invite you to share this time with us if it appeals to you.

While your current rent payment includes utilities (which we have calculated based on an average over the previous year's costs), energy prices are rising significantly each year. There may be times in the summer and winter when we will ask for an additional contribution should any utility bill increase exorbitantly.

Your room comes with furniture, and we ask that you take care not to damage any of it and that if you do, that you pay for its repair or replacement. There is limited room for additional furniture, and we have no storage space outside of your room.

You are welcome to use the house phone line for limited local calls. Please use other options (your own cell phone, prepaid calling cards or Voice Over IP) for long distance or extended local calls.

We enjoy hosting visitors from time to time—either for a meal or sometimes for a few days—and we invite you to do the same. In such cases we will all give each other notice and work out any necessary logistics.

Because Jillaine works at home during the day, please respect her needs for periodic privacy and quiet during this time. In addition, the house line is her business line during business hours.

We do not allow any smoking in the house or its immediate vicinity.

We are open to and encourage negotiation of additional agreements and courtesies as they might arise.

While it is our preference and request to resolve any conflicts directly and as soon as they occur, we recognize that from time to time incompatibility results in the inability for our living arrangements to continue. This has been extremely rare in the 11 years we have lived with housemates. But should such a circumstance occur, we (Philip and Jillaine), as leaseholders of this house, have the responsibility and the right to provide you with 30 days' notice; similarly, you have the responsibility and the right to provide us with 30 days' notice. At such a time, your last month's rent will be applied. Your security/cleaning deposit will be returned to you within 10 days of your departure, less any costs associated with loss or damage caused by you.

Example 3 House Rules

- 30-day notice on move-out or forfeit deposit (only exception is if the room is leased to next renter prior to move-out date).
- Deposit is returned in full after move-out if room is in move-in condition. Touch-up painting, cleaning and any repair fees will be deducted. (Please provide forwarding address.)
- Turn off lights when you leave a room.
- Always lock doors, check exterior porch door in the evening.
- Clean microwave oven after use and restore clock to "ready" status.
- Wipe down kitchen counters and sink after all food preparation and use of eat-in kitchen dining using appropriate cleaning materials.
- Use available and appropriate cleaning products frequently.
- No laundry past 9 pm—and remove laundry promptly from washer and / or dryer.
- Vacuum your room weekly.
- Do not drive nails into doors under any circumstances.
- Scrub clean and turn off natural gas grill and natural gas line after use and spray clean eating area if used.
- Notify owner of plans to entertain guests 24 hours in advance.
- Keep media room TV volume very low past 9 pm on weeknight evenings.
- In general—if you make a mess, clean it up.
- Do not alter / change or tamper with any house system (i.e., sound system, TV remote / cable box settings, phone, cable service, internet, electric, HVAC) unless your actions mitigate damage or if there is imminent danger.

Worksheet

What are the basic rules about using your home and things that a new housemate should know?

Do you have any pet peeves that you are aware of?
Write down any you know you have. (Of course, you don't have to have
pet peeves. The fewer you have, the easier it will be to live with you.)

Chapter 11

Daily Living, Sharing the Home

Good housemates cooperate as they deal with the day-to-day realities of living under one roof. They don't have to do everything the same way, but they need a general agreement about the home. All of these should be discussed in the interview process.

The common areas where you and your housemate interact are:

- Bills
- Sharing meals—or not
- Cleaning the kitchen
- General cleaning
- Managing personal property
- Guests

Generally, these are the areas that can cause conflict if there isn't agreement on how they should be managed.

The householder has the upper hand in establishing general policies. After all, it is her space, and she gets to decide whom she wants to live with. (In group households, the group may decide what the general policies are.) Any strong preferences that can't be adjusted for the comfort of the new housemate should be in the list of "must haves" or "can't live withs." Everything else can be discussed and decided on mutually. Use the worksheet at the end of this chapter to record your past experiences with daily living in a shared home. Writing down your experiences can help you clarify what you would like in your next shared living arrangement.

Bills

What household bills are there in addition to paying rent? When the householder decided on the rent, he determined whether the rent would include utilities and other house expenses. Any house expenses outside of the rent must be discussed and agreed upon in the interview. These expenses could include cable/Internet, heat/air conditioning, water and sewer, electricity, gas, parking, and cleaning. No housemate should impose on another a new charge or refuse to pay what was been agreed on at the outset. If the financial agreement needs to change, this should be discussed. If costs change due to outside circumstances, all the members of the household should be a party to deciding how to manage it. When Philip and Jillaine rented a room in their house they included the cost of heat, but in the interview they stated that if costs should go up, they expected the housemate to help pay the increased bill.

Some group houses choose to divide responsibility for the bills among the members, with each person having the bill in his or her name. Other houses keep the bills in the householder's name. This depends on the particular house-sharing arrangement.

Last but not least, a good housemate pays her bills on time.

Sharing Meals—or Not

The kitchen is the room that is used most by all members of the household. Everyone has to eat. But what and how individuals eat is extremely varied. What is normal to you may be totally foreign to someone else. Patterns are formed by family culture, health considerations, religion, attitudes toward cooking, and lifestyle. How do you want to share this space? Do you want to eat with your housemates, or do you want to be able to be independent at all times? Or are your preferences somewhere in between? Are you opening up your home to a home seeker for the express purpose of having someone to share meals with? This was the case for Adelaide. At the age of 75 she found herself overwhelmed with all the tasks of living alone. When she heard that I needed a place to live for the summer, she offered me a room in exchange for shopping and cooking dinner, which we ate together.

There are advantages and disadvantages to the various arrangements - what works for one person will be misery to another. It really depends on what you want. At one end of the spectrum is complete independence; at the other end is full community, with many variations in between.

Independence

One option is complete independence. When busy professionals share housing and have lives that include travel, eating out, and coming home at different times, independence is the arrangement that is the least complicated and easiest to manage. It is also the easiest when strangers are sharing housing.

In this arrangement, each person buys and keeps his own food in the house. Sections of the refrigerator, freezer, and cabinets can be assigned so that each person can easily see what food she has. Milk, soda, and other items that don't easily fit on shelves can be labeled with a black marker. One household uses cardboard boxes, and each person keeps his food in a box clearly marked with his name. Another household has two large refrigerators to keep everyone's food.

In all my shared housing, this option was my choice. Because I traveled for work frequently and liked to eat out with friends spontaneously, it simply wouldn't have worked to share food. The independence option sidesteps areas of potential conflict around money, time, and responsibility. On the other hand, it isn't very social or communal.

Community

The communal household shares the tasks of shopping, cooking, and cleaning up, as well as the cost of all the food that enters the house. It can be a huge time-saver, since the tasks are shared. It can also be a joy. Eating together is a basic human activity. People know each other, and relationships develop.

An example of communal living is Foundation Farm, a shared housing farm in New Hampshire that existed for 20 years or more. Housemates shared all food, including what the farm produced. In general, the home had four to six adults living there at one time. Each adult cooked one dinner a week. For the evenings when no one had responsibility, everyone was on their own to make their meals, including helping themselves to leftovers. Breakfast and lunch were always independently prepared. Everyone kept receipts when they went shopping, and at the end of the month, one person took all the receipts and figured out who owed whom to even out the bills. If someone wanted to buy himself a special treat, and it needed to be in the fridge, it was marked with that person's name so that the others would know it wasn't common property.

For meals, the cook chose what he wanted to cook. The person who cooked also did all the clean-up for the meal. This arrangement had the simplicity of ensuring that if the cook used every pot available, he would be also cleaning it. For everyone else, this arrangement meant one night in the kitchen, the other nights completely free.

In Washington, D.C., Jillaine and Phillip often had foreigners as housemates. Although sharing meals was not a requirement, they found that a pattern naturally evolved toward sharing meals together. With three people in the house, each person cooked for two nights a week. They didn't try to share the cost of food, but on the night that someone cooked for all, that person provided the meal from his or her personal larder. Jillaine says, "It was wonderful. We particularly appreciated learning about different cultures through the foods our housemates would cook and the conversations they would have. If someone couldn't be present on their night to cook, we would swap. Generally, everyone would have 24 to 48 hours' notice. Exceptions are okay when they are exceptions, but not when they are the norm." Breakfast and lunch were universally eaten independently.

The downside of communal eating is that because it makes you dependent on another person it can add enormously to the potential for conflict. It also ties you down on specific days and times, which doesn't work for some people.

Something in Between

Some households maintain independence of food ownership and occasionally choose to cook together. This might be by plan ("Let's have dinner together every Sunday") or may happen spontaneously. Sometimes two housemates are getting ready to cook at the same time and decide to pool their resources and make a meal together.

> In Connie's house, she and her housemate Bev are both established professionals in mid-life. They eat dinner together most nights, and each contributes to the meals without anyone keeping track of the money. As Connie says, "I don't want to be bothered by doing accounts. That would be a chore." Their method has evolved over the five years they have shared a home.
>
> In Shana's house, where food is kept independently, a housemate might decide to make a large soup or stew to share with the entire house. There is an understanding that the people eating should chip in some money to cover the cost of the food. They also keep a "blessings shelf." Food on that shelf is for anyone who wants it.

Some households share cooking basics that aren't used up quickly, such as spices, cooking oils, baking soda, and condiments. One household asks each member to chip in a certain amount of money per month that is kept in a kitty. When members buy items that are considered staples in that house, such as olive oil, baking supplies, paper goods, and cleaning supplies, they reimburse themselves from the kitty. For items over $10, permission must be given before kitty money is spent.

Some households share all food but eat independently. Linda and her goddaughter have evolved a system whereby each of them shops at a particular supermarket; there are certain foods that come from each market. They don't keep track of costs but keep an awareness of making an equal contribution to the larder. If they happen to be home at the same time, they might cook and eat together. This model probably wouldn't work for housemates who were strangers before moving in together, but it might work very well for adult family members who are sharing housing.

Cleaning the Kitchen

"Whose dirty dishes are these in the sink?" That is one of the more annoying housemate issues. Most mature adults recognize that cleaning up after you cook and washing your dishes is part of the deal. In one communal house, there was a rule that everyone cleans their own dishes "and one more." This rule generously recognized that occasionally a housemate would run out of the house and leave a coffee cup or a bowl in the sink with the intention of washing it later. In a different communal kitchen, each housemate owns his own dishes and utensils. Though this means that the house has no matched dinnerware, everyone always knows whose dishes are in the sink. In this household, they had trouble with one housemate who, despite repeated reminders to wash his dishes, just didn't do it. Finally, in frustration, one member bought a plastic tub and put this housemate's dirty dishes in the tub and on the back porch to get them out of the way. This is a creative way to deal with a source of irritation.

In Mike's house, he says, "[We have a] kitchen rule: 'I should come in, you should come in, and it should be as if no one has been there.'" He adds, "I have a good arsenal of cleaning products." In Chelsea's house of six housemates, each person in the house has a night during the week that is her "kitchen night." On kitchen night, that person is responsible for making sure that everything is put away, the sink is clean, and the floor is washed. As a result, every morning the kitchen is sparkling as the day begins.

In other households, cleaning the kitchen is part of the general cleaning work.

General Cleaning

Dirt: It is a fact of life. Spiderwebs, coffee rings, grit tracked in from outside, dust—it happens. Some people love to clean and some hate it. Some notice the speck on the countertop, others miss the dried toothpaste in the sink. Everyone thinks that their sensitivity to dirt is normal until they live with someone who is different.

The householder decides how the home is to be cleaned. This should be part of the interview. There are basically three options for cleaning: the householder takes care of the common rooms, everyone divides up the task, or someone is hired to do the cleaning. Each housemate cleans his own spaces, including a private bathroom if he has one.

Often in homes owned by the householder, the householder takes responsibility for cleaning the common areas, since it is his house and his furnishings.

When housemates share in the cleaning tasks of the household, they usually have some method for dividing up the tasks and rotating responsibility for them. In the house Sara lives in with six housemates, there are six areas of responsibility. Each person takes on responsibility for keeping that area clean. At the end of a month, a household member can request a rotation of duties.

In another house, tasks are placed on a "chore wheel" and the tasks rotate weekly so that no one person does the same task all the time. There is an additional rule that if a task isn't done until late in the week, the next person assigned to the task doesn't have to complete it.

In Sam's house, it was spelled out differently. "We had five chores for five people. The jobs and the person responsible were printed out in a table. Each week the job rotated. When the job was completed, the person doing it crossed it off the table. The table made it obvious if someone wasn't doing their job. If they ended up doing it so late as to make cleaning by the next person unnecessary, that person got a freebie."

In households of two people, the cleaning tasks might be more easily divided. It may not be necessary to have a formal system. This again depends on your preferences. In the apartment that Terry shares with his housemate-turned-good-friend, he says, "we'll suddenly announce 'Spring cleaning time!' and we both go to it."

The third method for managing the cleaning tasks is to hire someone to do it. This avoids most conflict about who is doing what and whether the tasks were completed on time and to everyone's satisfaction (assuming the cleaner is good). This is a cost that might be a part of the rent, be split between housemates, or, as in Deb's case, "I pay for cleaning in common areas and my spaces, but my housemate pays for the cleaning of his own space."

Possessions

The householder probably has a home with furniture, pots and pans, cutlery, and cleaning supplies. These will be used by housemates. And being used, they inevitably will be dropped, banged, scratched, spilled on, or otherwise exposed to the accidents of life. Some people are more clumsy than others, some are more observant than others. The householder must expect a certain amount of wear and tear. If there are possessions that are valuable—even if just of sentimental value—and their damage would be horrific and unforgivable, put them away where they can't be damaged.

Housemates who use things should be careful to respect the householders' requirements about how their possessions get used. If the householder always washes her good cooking knife by hand, dries it, and puts it in a wooden block, then that is how the housemate should use it. If she can't follow those requirements, she shouldn't use the knife. Anything that is damaged should be fixed or replaced. This is common courtesy. If someone broke something of yours, you would like to have it replaced, wouldn't you?

The home seeker also has possessions—sometimes many, sometimes very few. Whatever he wants to move into his room (assuming it isn't dangerous) is his own business. A different question is how the housemate's possessions might fit in the common spaces. Sometimes two people's possessions complement one another—one person may have a vacuum cleaner and another a toaster oven. Or one will have a couch and another will have a dining room table. When a householder has been in her home for a while, most likely it is fully furnished and there is no space for the home seeker's things besides her room. This should be talked about during the interview process. It is up to the home seeker to figure out what to do with possessions that won't fit in the home. In some cases there is a basement or attic for storage.

Some housemates, in their enthusiasm of moving into a new apartment, will decide to split the cost of small appliances, pots and pans, dishware, or other things the home needs. Don't do this. It makes it much harder to deal with moving out—whenever that happens. A better option is to make a list of what is needed and to split the list so that one housemate wholly owns one item each.

Some householders rent a room in their home and don't want any other rooms to be changed. That's fine. And some don't expect the home seeker to use any other rooms in the house but their own room and the kitchen. That's one way of sharing a house. But if the householder wants the home seeker to feel at home in the whole house and to use the common rooms, the householder may invite the home seeker to add something to the common areas—a piece of furniture or something on the wall. This is a symbolic gesture that invites the new member of the house to be a part of it.

Guests

There are guests who visit for a meal or an evening, and there are guests who stay overnight. In the interview process, householder and home seeker should talk about their desires and preferences for having people visiting the home. The interview conversation sets the expectations for managing guests in the house, including anticipated visits from significant others, friends, or family members. Children visiting a parent on a regular basis are housemates, not guests, and should be part of the interview process.

Some households plan social events together, inviting their friends to a party or weekly potluck. Other households don't socialize together but meet their friends outside of the home. Sometimes a housemate invites friends to the home when the householder is away. For instance, when Linda went on a trip, her housemate gave a little party. Or the householder might have a special event and ask that the housemates not be present. Mike says, "If I have a date that I'm entertaining at home, I announce it and the guys will vacate." It really depends on the household. In the communal household that Ann lived in, she says, "We welcomed guests. However, if a guest had a conflict with someone else in the household, that guest wasn't welcome."

There are two types of overnight guests: those visiting from somewhere else and sexual partners. Assuming that it is okay to have guests visiting from somewhere else, all residents should be informed right away so that they can say whether this is a problem for some reason. Plans for a visit should not be made until the visit is cleared with the housemates. Everyone should know when the visit is to occur. There is a common proverb: "Fish and guests have one thing in common. They both stink on the third day." This is well worth considering in planning on visitors.

> The first Thanksgiving weekend that Teresa shared a house with John, her parents came for Thanksgiving. This was okay for two days, but they didn't leave until Sunday. Teresa hadn't thought about the length of this visit and didn't feel that she could tell her parents to go when they clearly expected to stay for the whole weekend. John was very upset. It would have been much better if everyone has known ahead of time how long the visit would be.

The guest who shares your bed is a different category. A significant other who is part of your life when you are interviewing should be discussed, including how often you would expect that person to be in the house. Your housemate should not be surprised with this person's presence.

A new lover can upset a household even when this new person is liked and everyone is happy for the couple. When the boyfriend or girlfriend spends lots of time at the house, this person has become a de facto part-time housemate—

but one that the other members of the household did not interview and accept into their lives. This "extra" person is also not sharing the expenses. Resentment can blossom as the person uses hot water, heat, electricity, and other utilities that others are paying for. This tension need not become an outright conflict if everyone realizes what is happening and has a good conversation about how to manage it. Many households find a way to make an accommodation—the new person pays something for utilities, or isn't around quite so much, or the housemate spends more time at the other's place. This is a very good situation to remember the guideline "do it while it's easy." Communicate about the issue before it becomes a big deal. As experienced householder Lisa says, "When a guest has been in my home for four days, we need to have a conversation."

Living in Harmony

Paying bills, sharing the kitchen, managing the cleaning, using possessions, handling guests—these are the main components of the daily sharing of a dwelling. When these elements are handled as agreed upon in the interview process, the household can run smoothly and agreeably for all residents. These are the basics. When everyone honors the commitments made and takes responsibility for her part in the household, housemates can relax and enjoy the fact that they have a home in which they are comfortable. As life develops in the home, different activities emerge. Some households gather in a family room to watch football together, others decide to have a vegetable garden in their back yard. Some are always completely independent, with housemates rarely interacting. It all depends on what you want.

Worksheet

For each of the categories, consider your past experience (this can include family and/or significant others) and what you liked and didn't like about that experience. Then write down what you would like in your current or next shared housing arrangement

Bills
What did you like about it? What didn't you like?

Describe what you want for your next home sharing experience.

Kitchen
What did you like about it? What didn't you like?

Describe what you want for your next home sharing experience.

Kitchen Cleaning
What did you like about it? What didn't you like?

Describe what you want for your next home sharing experience.

General Cleaning
What did you like about it? What didn't you like?

Describe what you want for your next home sharing experience.

Possessions

What did you like about it? What didn't you like?

Describe what you want for your next home sharing experience.

Guests

What did you like about it? What didn't you like?

Describe what you want for your next home sharing experience.

Chapter 12

Guidelines for Happy Households

Though every household has its unique personality four guidelines for successfully sharing housing are universal. By following these guidelines, you will ensure that all the work you have put into finding a good housemate will pay off. You will be able to keep that good housemate by being a good housemate yourself. These guidelines apply equally whether you are the householder or the home seeker.

Guideline 1 The Golden Rule

Known as the Golden Rule, this ethic of reciprocity is commonly spoken of as "Do unto others as you would have them do unto you." Or in plain English: treat others the way you want them to treat you. If you expect to walk into a clean kitchen, don't leave your own plates in the sink. If you are sharing a bathroom with someone who has the same morning schedule, you have to figure out how to share it so that neither of you is stressed. If there is beer in the fridge and you don't have permission to take it, don't take it. If you come in late at night and everyone is asleep, don't make noise that would wake others. When housemate ads say they are looking for someone who is "respectful," this is what they mean.

This guideline also means recognizing that your housemate is different from you. You may not mind if she borrows some of your butter when you run out, but your housemate may mind very much if you do the same.

This is a rule that sometimes isn't as easy to follow as we might think it is. As human beings, we often have a hard time seeing how we affect others, so this leads to another guideline.

Guideline 2 Do It While It's Easy

"Do it while it's easy" means: don't allow small annoyances to build up. Unless you are an unusually easy-going person, it is inevitable that your housemate will do something at some point that bothers you. Don't ignore it. It will build up until it becomes a big thing. You will have an internal conversation with yourself, or actual conversations with others, until whatever the annoyance is has metamorphosed into an issue. There is a saying, "Don't make mountains out of molehills." It corrects the human tendency to exaggerate an issue. "Do it while it's easy" says, "communicate about the molehill while it is still a molehill." It may take some practice to recognize the difference between a small annoyance that you will forget—thus causing it to go away—and one that could become an issue.

Mention the annoyance as soon as you notice it. Using an "I" statement, tell your housemate how the annoyance affects you. For instance, "I don't like seeing sponges left in the sink," Or "I woke up last night when you slammed the door." Using an "I" statement is simply informing the other person about how his behavior affects you. You can follow the "I" statement with a request for different behavior—"I'd prefer it if they were squeezed out and put on the sink edge"—or you can wait for the person to respond. Many times the housemate simply didn't realize that there was an issue. So either the issue is quickly resolved or it involves a conversation to find resolution.

This rule goes hand in hand with the Golden Rule. By telling your housemate right away about the little thing that is annoying you, you are treating her as you would want to be treated. You would want to know about the little things that keep your housemate from being comfortable, especially if it is a simple fix.

Not everybody is comfortable mentioning an issue right away. Michelle says, "This is a really silly thing. Our housemate was given permission to use our stuff in the kitchen, but I found that every time I wanted to use this particular thing, it wasn't where it belongs because she was using it. It took me awhile to say something, and I just felt myself getting annoyed. I finally said something about it, and she went out immediately and bought her own since she realized she liked it so much."

Guideline 3 Your Room Is Your Own

In shared housing, your room is your haven. It is yours alone, and whatever you do in your room is your business unless it is bothering someone else. It should go without saying that no one should enter your room without permission, and you shouldn't enter anyone else's room without permission. In the eight years I lived in one apartment with housemates, I don't think any of them entered my room.

However, if what you are doing impinges on the rest of the house, then the first two guidelines trump this guideline. If others are affected by what you do in your room—for instance, playing loud music; leaving food around that attracts pests, be they ants or mice; or smoking in a non-smoking house—then your room is not your own. Jillaine and Phillip once had an infestation of roaches in a home that had previously not had them. After some investigating, they discovered that their housemate had a habit of leaving cookie crumbs and empty yogurt containers in his room. Once the housemate learned about the pests, he was more careful about keeping food out of his room.

Guideline 4 The "Incest" Taboo

The "incest" taboo is simply that. When living under the same roof, you must treat each other as family and not allow sex and sexual attraction to complicate the arrangement. A home should be a haven of safety and comfort, not the source of emotional highs and lows. The incest taboo creates familial comfort. With the incest taboo firmly in place, you can share housing very well with someone of either sex and of the same sexual orientation.

I owe the formulation of this rule to one of my former housemates. We lived together for many years and interviewed several home seekers together. Every now and then, he would have to make a decision about whether he wanted to date someone or have her as a housemate. Do not ever choose to live with someone because you "hope something will happen." This is a guarantee of disaster. Likewise, do not accept living with someone who you think might have a sexual interest in you. One straight female friend interviewed a straight man to rent the spare room in her house. While she didn't invoke the incest taboo in the interview, she nonetheless turned him down. She said, "I didn't like the vibe." After she turned him down, he asked her for a date. She said, "I knew that there was something not right there."

To be fair, occasionally or rarely, two housemates will fall in love, get married, and live happily ever after. If two housemates become a couple, they need to have an open conversation with each other and with their other housemates about what it means and how their relationship changes the housemate relationship. Certainly, if the couple should fall out of love, one or both of them will move out.

The Last Guideline Don't Overdo the Rules

These four guidelines—the Golden Rule, "Do it while it's easy," "Your room is your own," and the "incest" taboo—will help to ensure that you have a successful housemate relationship. These are guidelines, not rules; they offer flexibility and generosity. After all, you are living with people whose lives are dynamic and whose circumstances change.

There are households that have many rules about what to do and what not to do. The problem with lots of rules is that rules often have unexpected consequences. For example, imagine that you have a rule that overnight guests must be approved a week in advance. What do you do when a friend calls you at midnight because his car won't start and you are ten minutes away? Do you drive the friend an hour home, or do you let him crash on your couch to deal with the car in the morning? Crashing for the night makes sense, but the rule has been broken. The housemate who feels as if the rule has been transgressed might be upset, thus creating a source of conflict. The answer is not to create yet another rule. The answer is to have as few rules as possible.

Home should be a place of comfort, a place where you can be yourself. Minor adaptations for the comfort of your housemate are part of the give and take of sharing housing.

Exercise

Presented below are four scenarios that could occur when sharing housing. In each of the scenarios, consider what is going on for each of the housemates and what they should do. A commentary follows each scenario.

1.   When Glen moved into the house that Bill owned, Glen told Bill that he rarely ate at home, because he likes to eat out with friends. Bill said that he likes to have quiet time in the kitchen after a busy day of teaching fifth grade. They've been housemates for two months now and are getting along very well. Lately Bill has noticed that Glen is often home at dinnertime, lots more than what Bill had been led to expect when he invited Glen to move in. They talk as each makes his dinner. Tonight Bill was alone in the kitchen and halfway through his cooking when he heard Glen come in. He asked himself with irritation: "Why doesn't Glen leave me alone once in a while?" When Glen came into the kitchen, Bill greeted Glen warmly and asked him about his day. Glen hung out with him for the next hour.

    A. If you are Glen, what are you feeling/thinking?
    B. If you are Bill, what are you feeling/thinking?
    C. How would you apply the guidelines for successful home sharing to this situation?

This is an example of how people change according to the situation. Glen said in the interview that he eats out all the time. What he didn't realize was that he was doing it to avoid his old housemates. He genuinely likes Bill and is enjoying their blossoming friendship. Bill, too, is enjoying the friendship, but it's not leaving him with his quiet time. Initially, as he was getting to know Glen, he didn't realize he was losing that time. Now, it's beginning to wear on him.

    This is a housemate relationship that needs to have a conversation. It's a "do it while it's easy" situation. Bill needs to speak up about his desire to occasionally have some time to himself. Glen needs to respect this so that they can enjoy the time when they are together.

2. Beth, Amy, and Laurel share a nice condo in the suburbs of a major metropolitan area. They don't socialize outside the home, but at home they are friendly. One evening, Beth describes to both Amy and Laurel the arrangements she has made to get her car to the shop for its 50,000-mile maintenance the next morning. Amy offers to follow Beth to the mechanic's and give her a ride to her office.

> A. If you are Beth, what are you feeling/thinking?
> B. If you are Amy, what are you feeling/thinking?
> C. How would you apply the guidelines for successful home sharing to this situation?

Amy's offer is an example of the Golden Rule.

3. Eighty-two-year-old Rosemary is spry, sharp, and a little hard of hearing. Forty-three-year-old Jean is her housemate. When Rosemary's husband died two years ago, Rosemary discovered that she rather liked having the house to herself. However, she decided to rent a room in her house because she needed the additional income and some help. She was secretly relieved that there would be someone at home if she had an accident or medical emergency.

When Jean moved in, the two women had made an agreement that Jean would cook dinner five nights a week, Sunday through Thursday, in exchange for a low rent for her room. They had become quite good friends over the six months that Jean had lived there. Rosemary has encouraged Jean to take up her love of painting and to exercise. Two months ago, Jean started taking a painting class that conflicted with the housemates' usual dinner time one night a week. Nothing was said about it, and Rosemary simply cooked her own dinner that night. Today, Jean came home and announced that she has signed up for an aerobics class that meets on an additional night, also at their usual dinner time. Rosemary says nothing and an unusual silence makes them both uncomfortable.

A. If you are Rosemary, what are you feeling/thinking?
B. If you are Jean, what are you feeling/thinking?
C. How would you apply the guidelines for successful home sharing to this situation?

It seems that Jean is forgetting that she has a responsibility to Rosemary to cook five meals a week. Rosemary should have spoken up the first time that Jean broke the agreement. The fact that she didn't may have left Jean with the impression that it wasn't so important to Rosemary. Since Rosemary has been so encouraging, Jean thinks she will be pleased that Jean is taking action in ways that Rosemary would approve.

This is an example of how not speaking up in the first instance can cause problems later. At this point, Rosemary has to remind Jean of her responsibility to the basic agreement. Then they can negotiate an agreement that works for both of them.

4. Three days after Kate moved into a household of five people, Brian notices a strong odor of patchouli in the hall outside his room. He hates the smell because he associates it with a high school girlfriend. As he investigates, it seems that the smell gets stronger at Kate's door. He knocks on her door. When she opens the door, not only does he get a huge whiff, he can see that she is burning incense—the source of the smell. As it happens, when Kate interviewed, she said she likes to burn incense, and no one seemed to think that it was a problem. However, Brian wasn't at the interview. It was at a time when he couldn't make it, and he had trusted his housemates to make a good decision. He asks Kate to put it out.

A. If you are Brian, what are you feeling/thinking?
B. If you are Kate, what are you feeling/thinking?
C. How would you apply the guidelines for successful home sharing to this situation?

This example illustrates one of the problems with missing a housemate interview, when it would have been easy for Brian and Kate to discuss the incense issue. By missing the interview, Brian missed an opportunity to negotiate incense, though he might not have realized it was a problem. Because the smell travels beyond the walls of Kate's room, she is not completely free to do what she wants in her room. A possible compromise is to figure out what scents would not bother Brian.

Chapter 13

Managing Conflicts

If you have chosen your housemate carefully and you already have agreements on cleanliness, neatness, bills, noise, guests, personal property, and how the house is used, there shouldn't be any conflict that you can't manage within the agreements you have already made. When conflicts do occur, a few tools will be helpful.

The first step is realizing that a conflict exists. Sometimes this is a slow realization - something goes on that you didn't deal with when it was easy or that you hoped would not happen again. Other times, a conflict erupts suddenly.

One day at work, I got a phone call from our house cleaner, who reported that one of my cats had peed on my housemate Tim's brand-new bed. The house cleaner stripped the bed, and when I got home I put Tim's linens in the wash. Luckily, it hadn't soaked through to the mattress topper. When Tim got home, I gave him the bad news. He was furious and shouted, "You're buying me a new bed!!!" I knew he was overreacting, so I let him storm to his room, resolving to keep my cool. When he came back, he shouted, "You're buying me a new mattress pad from Ikea this weekend. I want it on the bed by the time I get home on Sunday." I said, "Can I just tell you what the house cleaner said?" He said to go ahead. First, I told him how sorry I was, and that I had no idea why it had happened. Then I told him that the house cleaner had stripped the bed and that it did not appear that it had penetrated through to the mattress topper he has on top of the mattress. I told him that I was washing his linens and that the door to his room, which was usually closed, had been open for some reason, allowing the cat to enter. At this, he shouted, "This is not my fault!!!" That's when I lost it myself and shouted back, "Well, guess what? It's not my fault either! And I do not need to be yelled at!" and stormed out. Less than a minute later, Tim was saying he was sorry he'd yelled at me. I said I was sorry I'd reacted the way that I did and acknowledged that if it had happened to me, I'd be angry too. Then we agreed that we should both be more vigilant about making sure that Tim's door is closed. And he said I didn't need to buy him a new mattress pad. Conflict resolved. As for the kitty, it was such unusual behavior that I decided to take him to the vet for a checkup, where he turned out to have a urinary infection.

This is a story of a housemate conflict that was resolved relatively quickly. In the midst of anger and upset, there was also:

- explanation,
- listening,
- problem resolution, and
- apologies.

At the conclusion of the incident, new procedures were agreed on to prevent the situation from happening again.

Sometimes you know ahead of time that you need to address an issue that has been building up for a while. Years ago, in college, I shared a house with four friends. One week, we needed to have a meeting. It was a big deal and was planned ahead of time. When we met, it turned out that everyone was irritated because they felt I wasn't doing my fair share of the cooking and cleaning. I was shocked. I simply had no idea that I hadn't been helping enough. We created a more formal schedule for the tasks that needed to be done, and I paid more attention.

Key Techniques

While conflict is never easy, think of it as a conversation that will make your home more comfortable for you. Keep that goal in mind. In a conflict mediation process, there are two key techniques that work remarkably well: one is using "I" statements, and the other is paraphrasing.

"I" Statements

"I" statements are exactly that. You describe how you are affected:

> "When I walk into the kitchen in the morning and see your dirty dishes in the sink, I'm annoyed."
> "I'm unhappy when I walk into the living room and see your stuff lying around."
> "I don't want to pay for the electricity that the air conditioner uses when it is left on and no one is in the room."

An "I" statement is your experience, plain and simple. It is the opposite of "you" statements, which often seem to be attacking the other person:

> "You never pick up after yourself."
> "Why can't you do the dishes?"
> "You always have an excuse for leaving the air conditioner on."

Use "I" statements to make it clear that you are speaking from your perspective. Avoid sentences with phrases such as "you never" or "you always," as these words are accusatory and will escalate the fight. They are usually exaggerations of the problem. Exaggerating leads to emotional reactions, which are not conducive to conflict resolution.

Paraphrasing

Paraphrasing is when one person repeats in his own words what the other has said. A paraphrase may start with, "Let me see if I understand what you said. You said that you don't take out the recycling because I don't put the newspaper in the recycling bin when I'm done with it" or "So you are telling me that you don't think it's such a big deal because it's only a couple of glasses and a plate." When you are listening in order to paraphrase, it prevents you from rehearsing how you will respond. It is easier to react, especially if you think that the person is wrong. Don't react. Remember that your goal is to find resolution, not to fan the flames of discord. Paraphrasing may feel silly, but do it anyway. It's remarkable how your ability to articulate the other person's perceptions will lower the temperature when there is a conflict. Often half the problem is resolved if the other person really feels heard. Make certain your housemate agrees that your paraphrase accurately expresses her thoughts and feelings.

When we actively try to understand another's point of view, we gain the other's willingness to listen to us. One of the habits in Stephen Covey's *The Seven Habits of Successful People* is "Seek first to understand, and then to be understood." It's worth reading his full description of this principle.

Use "I" statements and paraphrase until you and your housemate have a complete understanding of the issue. It usually doesn't take very long. Once you know about the issue from each other's perspective, you can find a resolution. You might agree to be more vigilant about the dishes, or to pay a larger portion of the electricity bill. Often the resolution is obvious. Sometimes it takes a compromise: both parties agree to adapt their expectations and behavior so that the other housemate is comfortable.

Final Thoughts

Apologies can also make a huge difference in a conflict. Heartfelt expressions of contrition—recognizing that you have done something that caused another unhappiness, whether or not you intended to, is a basic human interaction.

There is an important place for apologies in a housemate conflict.

Don't try to address a conflict through e-mail, instant messaging, texting, or posting complaints on forums. All these forms of communication can lead to misunderstandings that can make a conflict worse. Instead, talk about the conflict directly and in person. Set up a meeting to talk if more than one person is involved. If your conflict is just with one person, find a time to open up the topic. The worksheet at the end of this chapter can help you to plan what to say and how to say it.

Like the story that begins this chapter, conflicts happen. Face them and move through them quickly so that you can restore your comfort and can live peacefully at home.

Worksheet

*Use this worksheet in preparation for talking about a conflict
and documenting the resolution*

Before talking with your housemate

1. What is your experience of the issue? Write this as an "I" statement and be specific.

2. Is there a prior agreement or expectation about this? Describe your understanding.

3. How have you contributed to this issue? Consider how your behavior might be contributing to the problem.

After talking to your housemate

4. What is your housemate's perception of the issue?

5. What is the resolution that you agreed to?

Chapter 14

When It Isn't Working

In a successful housing arrangement, all residents feel comfortable. They greet each other with smiles and go about their normal lives. In an unsuccessful housing arrangement, there is stress and tension. At what point do you decide that the relationship isn't working and isn't going to work? The answer is: When you don't want to go home and you've tried to fix the problem.

Discovering that you and your housemate can't live together comfortably is an unhappy realization. It usually dawns slowly, as little things annoy you and don't get resolved. Efforts to resolve issues are rebuffed, ignored, or become a source of conflict.

Although the details are unique, the root cause of a housemate death spiral almost always comes from an incomplete and/or too-casual housemate selection process. Every story of a nightmare housemate I've heard can be traced back to how the housemates selected each other. Less horrific than the nightmare housemate, but also problematic, is the housemate who owes money or isn't following through on other expectations established as part of the housing arrangement.

Money

When a housemate falls behind on the rent or bills, trouble is brewing. Money between housemates should be handled right away. No bill should be unpaid for longer than a week without a conversation about why it's unpaid and how it will be paid. If you are the one owing the money, it is your responsibility to speak up about it and discuss the situation. If you are the one owed money, a simple reminder to your housemate should be sufficient to get paid.

If you are the householder and your housemate has fallen behind on the rent and bills, don't let her fall behind longer than a month. Since she paid her last month when she moved in, you are covered for just one month. If she can't catch up, ask her to leave at the end of the month. Debts that mount up are a major source of stress. The longer you wait, the less likely it is that you will be paid. If your housemate has fallen on hard times, telling her to move out makes her life more difficult. However, your relationship is based on sharing the cost of housing. If you aren't being paid and you ignore that fact, you simply allow the situation to get worse.

Unmet Expectations

During the interview process, you and your housemate established certain expectations for how you would live under the same roof. If the reality is different from those expectations, someone is likely to be unhappy.

Sometimes expectations aren't met because of life changes. For instance, in the interview the home seeker may have described his nine-to-five job and said that he would be leaving the house Monday through Friday at 7:30 a.m. and wouldn't get home until 7 p.m. at the earliest. Then he changes jobs and starts to telecommute three days a week. Suddenly, he is home for those three days, and the privacy and silence the householder expected is gone. Or perhaps the householder offered a reduced rent in exchange for having a meal cooked three nights a week, but then the housemate gets a job waitressing for five nights a week, so she's not cooking the meals. There are lots of ways that an original agreement might be altered because of changing life circumstances. Negotiate these changes as soon as they come up. Remember to "Do it while it's easy."

Sometimes it is not possible to come to a workable new arrangement. In that case, it is time to end the relationship, recognizing that it no longer serves both of you. There should be no blame under these circumstances—life happens.

Some people don't take their responsibility as a housemate seriously. A housemate who doesn't live up to agreements made during the interview is a problem. Whether the weekly cleaning chore is neglected, the dishes are left in the sink, or a boyfriend is at the house every night, minor and major transgressions build tension in a relationship. If you have made honest efforts to communicate with the housemate and the housemate isn't adjusting his or her behavior to accommodate you (the Golden Rule), then it is time to think about having the housemate move out. When you get to the point where you are either avoiding your housemate or fighting with him, it's time to end the relationship.

Poor Selection Process

The most common mistake home sharers make is failing to follow a judicious and careful selection process. This happens because of inexperience, assumptions, and/or desperation.

Inexperience

Inexperienced home sharers may not realize the importance of the selection process. They may not realize what their own requirements are for a housemate, they may accept the person at face value, they may figure that they will play it by ear as it goes along and work it out as the time comes, and/or they may not check references. Any of these oversights could lead to a mismatch in housemates.

Assumptions

Making assumptions leads to trouble.

Adrienne needed a new housemate. She says about her ad, "I wasn't super descriptive. I got turned off by ads looking for their new best friend, so I wrote something simple, just describing the physical aspects of the apartment." Adrienne chose Jane, who was looking for a space because her boyfriend had asked her to move out for the time being. They didn't have an extensive interview. "I wasn't on alert or anything. She was pretty quiet, not animated. I expected I'd keep to myself and she would too and we would co-exist." It didn't work out. Adrienne says, "She would lock her room even when we would both be home. She would text me rather than talk to me. At one point, she realized I had replaced something of hers that I ate. She sent a really nasty e-mail. Seemed as if she decided then I was an awful person. After that she wouldn't respond to me at all, just go straight to her room, and avoided me completely." The end came when Jane announced that she was moving out.

Adrienne had made the assumption that Jane would be quiet. She also made a few mistakes in her selection process. She didn't describe in her ad what she was looking for in a housemate, she didn't check references, and she didn't find out why the boyfriend had asked Jane to move out.

Sometimes moving in with a friend, relative, or colleague turns out to be a mistake. While it is natural to assume that the person you already know and like will be a good housemate, living together is quite different. You share responsibility for your home and you see each other daily. Potential housemates should be selected after having a thorough discussion of how the house-sharing arrangement will work, comparing "must haves" and "can't live withs" (Chapter 3) before agreeing to live together. You may have quite different expectations about what it means to be housemates and very different habits at home than at work. Make sure it is a good match before you agree to live together. A bad match can cost you a friendship, a family rupture, or a job.

Desperation

Housing in some markets is so tight that home seekers often feel desperate, afraid of having nowhere to live or imposing on friends a little too long. This inevitably results in a poor selection process.

Meg is a 20-something entrepreneur who makes purses and accessories. On moving to a new city, she took an expensive sublet. One day, her landlord told her she had two and a half weeks to find a new place. Meg began to panic when the desirable postings on craigslist would disappear before she had a chance to interview for them.

One place she looked at was on the edge of town, with two men. One owned the apartment; the other rented from the first one. The room had furniture—a plus, since she had none—consisting of a bed, a desk, a lamp, and a scale. She looked at it and thought, "Well, this is survival, and it will do." So she moved in. Looking back, she says, "It was pretty reckless. I just did it. I'm pretty surprised I did it."

The situation slowly deteriorated over a winter. One issue was cleanliness. The two guys did not clean as much as Meg would have liked. The refrigerator got really disgusting. There was often rancid food in it. At one point, the householder offered to reduce Meg's rent in exchange for cleaning the bathrooms and the kitchen. Though it only took 45 minutes a week, Meg says, "I ended up feeling like the maid." Meg also became less friendly as it became clear that the householder was not a "respectful or courteous person." At some point, she realized that she needed to find another place to live, and soon after that she moved out. She found a good arrangement, having learned some lessons about "survival."

Feeling desperate—scared of not having a roof at all, or of not having a housemate to help pay the bills—can create bad situations. It is much better if you are able to avoid making decisions out of desperation. If you are the householder, leave the room unrented rather than allow someone about whom you have reservations to move into it. If you are the home seeker and you take a room in a situation that isn't up to your standards, recognize that it is temporary and keep looking for a better arrangement.

One way to avoid that scared, desperate feeling is to make contingency plans. If you are renting out a room in your home, have an emergency fund so that you can cover costs for a short period. If you are looking, investigate temporary options with friends or family ahead of time. Giving people a chance to think about offering you their guest room or couch in the future is much better than creating an emergency. This is another example where it is better to "do it while it's easy." A hypothetical "If I were stuck, would it be possible for me to crash with you?" feels quite different than "I need a place to sleep tomorrow!" When you give others time to consider a future possibility, they can make adjustments more easily.

Making the Decision

When things are not going well in a shared living arrangement, you don't want to make a decision based on the emotion of a moment.

Can It Be Fixed?

Before you decide that a situation can't be rescued, give it some thought at a time when you are not feeling desperate or angry. You don't want to make such an important decision without rational thought. Talk to a respected friend or colleague about the problem to get some objectivity. Talk and think through the problems you are having with the situation to decide whether it's something that can be fixed—by talking to your housemate, compromising on certain things yourself, or making other changes. Use the worksheet at the end of this chapter to sort out your thoughts. If you decide to talk to your housemate, you can use what you've written as a guide.

When the Answer Is "No"

It's a good idea to end a housemate relationship before it is so bad that everyone is miserable. The realization that you dread seeing a housemate, or that you don't want to go home, usually starts with a fleeting thought. Notice this little voice before it becomes a shout. At first it will be easy to push away and silence. "It's not that bad," you might say to yourself. Denial is a powerful psychological state, and many people can deny that things are bad for far too long, sometimes until the situation becomes unlivable. Don't do this to yourself.

A bad situation doesn't magically get better. If your best efforts to communicate and find a comfortable way to live with your housemate are not working, it's time to make a change. It's unfortunate and not much fun. Facing the need for a change is not pleasant; talking to the housemate about the change isn't fun. But you have to do it.

You need to take action, and that either means finding a new place to live or telling a housemate to go. It is good to have a clear idea about who stays and who goes. When the householder owns the home, this is easy. When it's a place that all are renting, who "owns" the lease becomes a stickier issue and can contribute to the conflict of the ending.

When the householder asks a housemate to leave, the decision must be clear and firm. If the relationship has deteriorated, both parties might be ready to dissolve the arrangement, but there might also be resistance—it's hard to move. If possible, come to an agreement on when the housemate will move out. If you can't agree, tell the housemate when you expect him to be gone.

When the ending occurs because the relationship has eroded, the transition out of the home is an uncomfortable period. In fact, the experience of a relationship deteriorating and the unpleasantness of evicting a housemate or having to find another place to live can create such a powerful experience that people decide they will never, ever, live in shared housing again. Though understandable, this is a false conclusion. It just wasn't the right situation.

Worksheet

Use this worksheet as preparation for a conversation to see if you can come to new agreements that will enable you to live together comfortably

1. List the things that your housemate is doing/not doing that are making you unhappy.

2. Describe how these affect you.

3. Put yourself in your housemate's shoes. What do you do/not do that makes your housemate unhappy?

4. Do you have a proposal for how the situation can be resolved?

Plan to have a conversation with your housemate.

Chapter 15

Moving Out

Shared housing is rarely a permanent arrangement, so it is inevitable that at some point the relationship will end. Life brings changes. Whether it is a new job in a different location, moving home to care for a parent, moving in with a significant other, or any of the many other ways that circumstances can change, when things shift, it is likely that the shared-housing arrangement no longer serves its purpose. It is time to move on.

These endings should be relatively easy. The new direction of the housemate is something to celebrate. However, there can be a conflicting emotional component. It is hard to be left behind, even when one understands and applauds the new directions. Those staying behind might be sad, anxious about the change, and/or mad. Little things can become irritants that were previously overlooked. Housemates might distance themselves or they might cling. Don't be surprised if these changes start happening. Remember the guidelines for living together and be kind to one another. Don't turn a happy ending into an unhappy ending.

When moving out, the housemate informs the householder of the date of the move with at least a month's notice. This gives the householder time to find a new housemate for the room. Since the householder is likely to be interviewing and wanting to show the room, both parties need to make an agreement about when the room can be shown. If you are moving out, be courteous to the householder by keeping your space clean and tidy in order to allow the householder to show the room at its best.

The mechanics of moving out involve rent, the security deposit, bills, and possessions. The housemate who is moving out won't have to pay the last month of rent since it was paid when he moved in. Bills need to be sorted out. Because some bills will come in after the housemate has moved out, there should be a plan for how to handle them. The security deposit is reimbursed only after the housemate has fully moved out and all bills are accounted for. If you've been living together for a while, it is a good idea to sort through kitchen equipment together. It's easy to forget who owns what if everyone has used the pots and pans, spatulas, and knives. The same is true for any other furniture, appliances, and things. (See the checklist at the end of this chapter.)

On moving day, housemates can help each other or not. If the person moving out has other people helping and there are possessions in the house that aren't just in the person's room, it is a good for the householder idea to be around. A zealous friend of the person moving out can misinterpret directions and put the wrong chair in the moving van.

Endings can be abrupt, or sad, or joyful, or empty. Some housemates walk out of each other's lives without any further connection. Other housemates continue to be dear friends. Some houses have reunions celebrating the friendships that started in shared housing and continue. Some purposely go and visit their former housemates. It all depends on the nature of the relationship.

Worksheet

Use this checklist you can use to track and document the steps necessary to completing a housemate transition. A copy can be given to the person moving out, so that everyone has the documentation

Moving Date:

Separating household goods: (Check when completed)

[ ] Kitchen (pots, pans, utensils, dishes, glasses, etc.)
[ ] Living room/family room (furniture, audiovisual equipment, movies/games, etc.)
[ ] Closets (off-season clothing, other stored stuff)
[ ] Bathroom (toiletries, medicines, first aid equipment)
[ ] Outdoor stuff (garden tools, shovels, rakes, etc.)
[ ] Storage areas

Address Change/Forwarding Address

_____

_____

_____

Bills

Type of Bill	Paid Up (most recent dates)	Outstanding (amount prorated)	Check when paid
Electric			
Internet/Cable			
Heat/AC			
Water			
Other			

House keys returned

Date: _____

Security Deposit

Amount: _____

Less bills and cleaning: _____

Total returned to housemate: _____

Date: _____

Conclusion

Sharing housing offers so much. It offers relief from the strain of housing costs and the advantage of living in better housing than you can afford alone. This is no small matter. Many of the people interviewed for this book turned to sharing their homes out of economic necessity. What they found, when they were careful in the process of selection and interviewing, is that they liked the shared living and the social connection of having housemates.

The process of finding a housemate can be an emotional time. It is, by definition, a time of transition when there is lots of uncertainty. As you navigate the process of interviewing potential housemates, you may find yourself alternately excited, exhausted, expectant, and anxious. You may wonder if you are ever going to find the right person. You may be tempted to relax your criteria. You may be tempted to accept the first person you talk to, or the one who "seems to be okay." Making a premature decision will lessen the tension of the uncertainty and transition, but you owe it to yourself to stick to your criteria and trust that you will find a suitable housemate.

By following the steps in this book, you will develop a housemate relationship. You start out unsure of whom you might meet and whom you will end up knowing as a housemate. When you start out, it can be scary. It can also be exciting, an adventure. Whatever the feeling, there is a huge question mark. "What if I don't find anyone?" "Who would want to live with me?" "Where will I be living?" "What if we don't get along?" Even if you are considering living with a friend, you don't know the person as a housemate. What you have learned here is that, before you start looking, you need to sit down and figure out what you are looking for. You aren't simply going to leave it all to chance and accept the first person you encounter. You are going to have criteria: a way to judge whether this person is for you.

With your criteria in hand, you write your ad, or start looking at ads. The first contact—by e-mail or telephone—starts the relationship. It builds as you have a telephone interview. In that interview, as you exchange information about your "must haves" and "can't live withs," you begin to get a sense of the other person. Then you actually meet for the in-person interview. This is where you discuss those things that are on your "like to have" list. You ask all the questions you can think of and you share your expectations of how sharing a home would work. Each step tells you more about your potential housemate and each step offers an opportunity to stop the process and walk away from this potential housemate. All through this process you are paying attention to your instincts and being realistic about what you can expect from a shared housing arrangement. All through this process you are honest, real, and authentic.

There are so many ways that the housemate arrangement can bring benefits. Sharon found a housemate with whom to eat occasional meals. Mike discovered the companionship of watching the game together. Theresa enjoys the sister-like relationship she has developed with her housemate. Whatever it is for you, however you want to live, you now know how to find and keep good housemates.

Use this process.

Visit us and tell us how it goes at http://www.sharinghousing.com

Resources

Finding a housemate

Craigslist: www.craigslist.org
   The largest resource for posting and looking for housemates. Free to post ads. Prone to scammers. Read the warnings and follow them.

CoAbode: www.coabode.org
   For single-mothers, a database matching service. National in scope.

Roommates Wanted: http://roommateswantednyc.com
   In New York City, regularly scheduled meet ups in clubs and bars where those looking for housemates can meet in person. Considering expanding to other cities.

NIH housing: http://teledirectory.nih.gov/servDet.php?ser=144

   National Institutes of Health list housing available. Check universities, teaching hospitals, research centers and other local institutions that have interns, students and other short-term professionals.

Managing Money

Housemate's Companion: http://www.housematescompanion.com/
   PC based software for housemates to manage bill paying and other expenses.

State housing boards:
   http://portal.hud.gov/portal/page/portal/HUD/states
   Find out what the laws in your state are about holding security deposits.

Home Share Programs

There are non-profit agencies that match householders with homeseekers, usually for help around the household in exchange for housing.

HomeShare International: www.homeshare.org
   Homeshare International encourages younger people to houseshare with older people, providing some help in the home in exchange for free - or a discounted - rental. Umbrella organization for homeshare programs worldwide. Based in England.

National Shared Housing Resource Center:
http://www.nationalsharedhousing.org/
   Website has information about shared housing programs in the United States. Searchable by state.

About the Author

Annamarie Pluhar became an expert on sharing housing through personal experience combined with expertise in group process and dynamics. A facilitator and training professional, she has worked with clients in Fortune 100 firms as well as non-profits. Early in her career, she was a consultant with Rath & Strong Inc., on the vanguard of the Total Quality movement. She has trained hundreds of cross-functional teams in problem-solving, interpersonal relationships, and teamwork. Currently, Annamarie designs and delivers training for corporate clients and federal agencies. She is a graduate of Vassar College and holds a Masters in Divinity from the Episcopal Divinity School. Annamarie is the owner of Pluhar Consulting. (www.pluharconsulting.com)

Annamarie offers workshops and coaching to support individuals in their quest for good housemates. The website SharingHousing.com contains articles, links to resources, a personal questionnaire and all the worksheets. She can be reached at: Annamarie@sharinghousing.com